TEA
GARDEN

Growing Your Own
TEA
GARDEN

The Guide to Growing and Harvesting Flavorful Teas in Your Backyard

JODI HELMER

Growing Your Own Tea Garden

CompanionHouse Books™ is an imprint of Fox Chapel Publishers International Ltd.

Project Team
Vice President—Content: Christopher Reggio
Editor: Colleen Dorsey
Copy Editor: Katie Ocasio
Design: Llara Pazdan
Index: Jay Kreider

ISBN 978-1-62008-322-2

The Cataloging-in-Publication Data is on file with the Library of Congress.

This book has been published with the intent to provide accurate and authoritative information in regard to the subject matter within. While every precaution has been taken in the preparation of this book, the author and publisher expressly disclaim any responsibility for any errors, omissions, or adverse effects arising from the use or application of the information contained herein.

Fox Chapel Publishing
903 Square Street
Mount Joy, PA 17552

Fox Chapel Publishers International Ltd.
7 Danefield Road, Selsey (Chichester)
West Sussex PO20 9DA, U.K.

www.facebook.com/companionhousebooks

We are always looking for talented authors. To submit an idea, please send a brief inquiry to acquisitions@foxchapelpublishing.com.

Printed and bound in China
25 24 23 22   6 8 10 9 7 5

DEDICATION

For my late grandmother, Veronica Thomas, who always made sure the kettle was on.

ACKNOWLEDGMENTS

Writing a book is a lot like brewing the perfect cup of tea: it takes the right ingredients and enough time to steep.

I'm grateful to Diane Daniel for introducing me to Bud Sperry at Fox Chapel Publishing and trusting good things would happen, and thankful that Bud believed in this idea and encouraged me to turn a passion into a manuscript. My dear friends Megan Bame, Heather Rice Books, Polly Campbell, Kate Hanley, Wendy Helfenbaum, Beth Howard, Kelly James, Judi Ketteler, and Rosie Molinary, and my family, Hank and Dianne Helmer, Shannon Helmer, and Charlotte McKinnon, supported me during the writing process.

My final and most heartfelt thanks is for my husband, Jerry, who is my favorite person to share a pot of tea with.

CONTENTS

PLANT INDEX

TEA (*Camellia sinensis*)

LEAVES

FLOWERS

FRUITS

ROOTS

INTRODUCTION

Some of my earliest and fondest childhood memories involve tea. My grandmother used to pour us each a cup of tea in her no-nonsense mugs, filling hers with steaming black liquid and a splash of milk, and preparing mine in reverse—a full cup of milk with just a splash of tea. We'd dunk homemade peanut butter cookies in our mugs and declare it a tea party.

While my tea preferences have changed— now, I prefer a strong, bitter cup of black tea, no milk, first thing in the morning; mint tea in the evenings; and something sweet, floral, and iced when it's sweltering outside—my love affair with tea has endured (and I still enjoy the occasional tea party, especially one that includes a fancy hotel and finger sandwiches). There is something so soothing about a cup of tea—the way its warmth transfers from the mug to your hands, how the scent of it is like aromatherapy, how a sip

is both familiar and new, the way you can put together just the right variety to fit the mood or fix what ails you.

Despite being a lifelong tea drinker, it had never occurred to me to grow all of the ingredients to make my own tea. The inspiration hit three years ago at a garden center where, standing in front of vast metal racks filled with peppermint, spearmint, chamomile, lavender, and lemon balm, I thought, "This looks a lot like the tea aisle at the supermarket." An image of a backyard tea garden flashed in my mind. Cue a cart filled with herbs and some bags of soil, and a few hours later I had all the makings of a great cup of tea right outside my back door. Every time I head outside to pick a fresh cup of tea, I remember my grandmother and feel a sense of gratitude for the continued comfort this ritual she taught me has brought me over the years.

This is the last time I saw my grandmother before she passed away—and she was enjoying a cup of tea, as always.

Judging from the explosion of options in the grocery store aisle, I know I am not the only one with affection for tea. Maybe you brew a cup of tea in the morning for a quick pick-me-up, use an herbal blend to ease digestive upset, or wind down with a steaming mug before bed. Maybe you host tea parties for the children in your life or your sewing circle or book club. Even if you are an old hand at growing tomatoes or herbs like basil and rosemary, it may not have ever occurred to you that your tea could come from your own yard, too. Instead of reaching into the cupboard for a supermarket tea bag, you can plant a tea garden and then enjoy clipping fresh herbs such as chamomile, lemon balm, basil, and peppermint for your own signature brews.

A tea garden provides instant access to fresh, flavorful herbs and allows you to get creative, mixing different plantings to create one-of-a-kind blends. And while it might seem daunting or fancy, growing the ingredients for tea is actually a great project for both beginners and experienced gardeners. Most herbs are easy to grow (most will thrive in pots on a sun-drenched windowsill), and making flavorful tea can be as simple as steeping a few freshly plucked leaves in boiling water or as complex as drying herbs and combining multiple ingredients to make custom brews. Whether you've never tended to a plant before or have a large garden and want a new hobby, starting a tea garden and sipping fresh, flavorful garden-to-teacup brews is a great way to embrace your fondness for this classic drink.

Disclaimer: This book is not a field guide; it's not intended to diagnose, treat, or cure any disease. I am a gardener and tea drinker, not a doctor or nutritionist. Although I did extensive research to ensure accuracy, you must make sure to positively identify all plants before eating leaves, flowers, fruits, and roots. Some wild plants are poisonous or can have adverse effects. Avoid consuming any unfamiliar plants. Consult with qualified health professionals to verify the health benefits and safety of consuming plants.

CHAPTER 1

A BRIEF HISTORY OF TEA

In this chapter, we'll take a look at where tea comes from, how it spread across the world and across the centuries, and what the tea landscape looks like today. By knowing the history of our preferred beverage, we can make informed choices about what we sip and why we want to sip it.

Tea has been cultivated for centuries, with the earliest records dating back to 2732 BC, when, according to legend, Emperor Shen Nung first drank tea after leaves from a *Camellia sinensis* bush— that is, the tea plant—drifted into his pot of boiling water. More reliable records show that tea was included in the medical text *De Materia Medica*, which was first published around 200 BC.

As tea started becoming more popular as a drink, not just a medicine, the cultivation, harvesting, and processing of *Camellia sinensis* started. During the Tang Dynasty (618–906 AD), often referred to as the classic age of tea, the botanical beverage became known as the national drink of

De Materia Medica has been published in many languages throughout the centuries, but it always contained useful information about helpful plants—including tea.

What Is a Tisane?

Some of the most popular "teas" are not tea at all. True tea is made from the leaves of the *Camellia sinensis* plant; herbal teas, including popular brews such as chamomile and peppermint, are considered tisanes.

Tisanes (pronounced ti-ZAN) are made from ingredients such as herbs, flowers, fruits, bark, and roots but no white, green, black, or oolong teas. (The French word for "herbal infusion" is *tisane*.) Rooibos (pronounced ROY-boss), also known as African red tea or red bush tea (because it's made from a South African rooibos plant), and yerba maté (pronounced YER-ba MAH-tay), a South American botanical brewed from a plant in the holly family, are also considered tisanes.

Unlike true tea brewed from *Camellia sinensis* leaves, which contain up to 90 milligrams of caffeine per 8-ounce (240ml) cup, tisanes are caffeine free. These teas, also called infusions or botanicals, can be sipped hot or iced.

Rooibos creates a beautiful red tea.

Saichō first planted tea seeds in his monastery in Japan, Enryaku-ji, which you can still visit today.

China; tea was sipped and savored from the Imperial Palace to rural villages. Tea also became the centerpiece of spiritual rituals. During the Tang Dynasty, Buddhist monk Lu Yu wrote *Ch'a Ching*, a tea treatise that centered Buddhist, Taoist, and Confucian teachings around traditional tea ceremonies.

Another Buddhist monk, Saichō, is credited with introducing tea to Japan in the ninth century. It's believed that the monk fell in love with tea while studying in China and brought *Camellia sinensis* seeds back to his monastery in Japan. There, the delicate green tea leaves were ground into powder, called *matcha*, which remains popular in Japan and worldwide.

Toward the end of the seventeenth century, camel trains operating along the

The Buddhist monk Saichō, pictured, introduced tea to Japan in the ninth century.

The Dutch East India Company used ships like these to develop and dominate the tea trade between Asia and Europe.

At first, tea was expensive and therefore only enjoyed by the rich.

Silk Road transported tea between China and Russia. In 1610, the Dutch East India Company brought the first shipments of tea to Europe. The beverage became popular in cities, including Amsterdam, and, before long, shipments were making their way from Dutch ports to the rest of Europe, including England, where the piping-hot beverage was first served to the public in 1657. Thanks to the high price of tea, it was enjoyed only by the royal and aristocratic classes. It wasn't until a hundred years after the first tea was imported to England that tea houses and tea gardens started popping up around London, and tea became the national drink of the British Isles. So, while England might have a well-deserved reputation for serving high tea—with crumpets, of course—the British were in fact late adopters of tea culture, and some of their knowledge of tea cultivation and processing were gathered using questionable methods.

An English afternoon tea, complete with scones, finger sandwiches, and pastries, is a treasured cultural activity in the country today.

In the 1700s, the British East India Company purchased a tea factory in Macao, China, and dominated the tea trade, exploiting its trading position for profit and political power. England was reluctant to depend on China for its tea, however, so in 1848 the British East India Company sent botanist Robert Fortune on a covert mission to China to collect *Camellia sinensis* seeds and plants while gleaning knowledge about how to grow and process the beverage. Fortune disguised himself and snuck into the interior region of China—an area forbidden to outsiders—and shipped 20,000 tea plants to India, where the species was tested in gardens across the nation, including the now-iconic tea regions of Assam and Darjeeling. The British government started developing tea estates across India, ending their reliance on China for tea.

Tea pickers are hard at work in the state of Assam, India.

Iconic in American history, the Boston Tea Party treated tea as a symbol of oppression.

Just as Holland introduced England to tea, Dutch settlers also brought tea to America. The upper class who settled in New Amsterdam, later renamed New York, started drinking tea in the 1600s. The British East India Company secured a monopoly on tea sales in the American colonies after British parliament passed the Tea Act on May 10, 1773. The legislation angered colonists, and, on December 16, 1773, a group calling themselves the Sons of Liberty boarded ships anchored in the Boston Harbor and dumped 92,000 pounds of tea into the water. The event came to be known as the Boston Tea Party.

Pressure from independent tea merchants like Richard Twining uncovered corruption within the British East India Company and put pressure on the British government to

Twinings, founded by an independent family of tea merchants who ultimately helped end the monopoly on the tea trade, remains one of the most successful and iconic British tea brands today.

end the monopoly on the tea trade. The campaign was successful, and the British East India Company folded in 1874, opening the door for America to import tea directly from China. Clipper ships began transporting the commodity across the ocean.

Worldwide, China still dominates tea production, harvesting more than 1.8 million tons of tea each year. In addition to China, the rest of the top ten tea-producing countries are India, Kenya, Sri Lanka, Turkey, Indonesia, Vietnam, Japan, Iran, and Argentina. The United States might not be a top cultivator of *Camellia sinensis*, but it is a significant importer.

Approximately 80 percent of Americans are tea drinkers. Nationwide, we consumed 84 billion servings of tea—almost 4 billion gallons (15 billion liters)—in 2016, making the United States the third largest importer of tea in the world, according to the Tea Association of the USA. Americans prefer their tea black or iced, but with more than 3,000 varieties of tea available, the options are almost limitless. Thanks to strong demand, US growers are experimenting with the crop and producing small-batch artisanal teas with some success.

Teas and infusions are incredibly popular in the United States, with a large variety available on standard supermarket shelves.

The rolling, stepped hills of Chinese tea plantations are where the most tea is produced in the world.

A LOCAL TEA MOVEMENT IS BREWING

Tea is growing—literally—in the United States. Minto Island Growers started growing *Camellia sinensis* on a half-acre plot in Salem, Oregon, hand-picking and processing the tender leaves to make small-batch tea. The interest in their domestic tea was so strong—the loose-leaf black, green, and oolong teas were selling out within weeks of their spring production—that husband-and-wife growers Elizabeth Miller and Chris Jenkins planted 20 additional acres of *Camellia sinensis* between 2016 and 2017, selling upward of 100 pounds (45 kilograms) of organic teas under the Minto Island Tea Co. brand. Miller told NPR, "It's the energy and enthusiasm from consumers that's propelling us forward. People are really excited to have tea that is US-grown."

The Charleston Tea Plantation in Charleston, South Carolina, has been growing tea since 1987 and was the sole commercial tea grower in the nation for a long time. Now, the US League of Tea Growers reports that there are sixty farms in fifteen states growing *Camellia sinensis*. Most were started in 2000 or later, and several, including Table Rock Tea Company, The Great Mississippi Tea Co., and Virginia First Tea Farm, are less than five years old as of this writing. The US League of Tea Growers has referred to the growing interest in domestic tea production as "an exploration into a brand new terroir."

The increase in US tea farms doesn't mean there is an increase in domestic tea production—yet. It takes at least three years for *Camellia sinensis* to mature, which means farms that started growing the niche crop after 2015 are not harvesting enough leaves to meet the demand for local teas. It takes

A massive quantity of leaves is required to produce tea.

What Is Yaupon?

A debate rages about whether this native plant should be called tea. Yaupon (pronounced YO-pon) has a native range from North Carolina to Texas and the distinction of being the only native North American plant that contains caffeine.

Native Americans used yaupon holly (*Ilex vomitoria*) to brew tea, but the plant fell out of favor around the time of the Civil War. Yaupon, also called cassina, is similar in both flavor and caffeine content to black tea. Southern growers are working hard to bring back yaupon tea, but purists argue that because the brewed beverage isn't made from *Camellia sinensis* leaves, it cannot be considered tea.

the leaves from almost 20,000 *Camellia sinensis* plants to produce 5,000 pounds of tea.

Many up-and-coming tea growers are testing the viability of *Camellia sinensis* in their regions. The shrub prefers mild climates with significant rainfall and well-drained, acidic soil. It tends to grow well in the South—New Orleans is the same latitude as tea-growing regions in southern China. Even growers in places like Michigan and Oregon are experimenting with the crop.

Tea grown in the United States is more expensive. Labor costs are much higher than in traditional tea-producing countries, where growers might earn less than $20 per week, making domestic tea a high-end artisanal product. Compared to supermarket tea bags, which can retail for as little as $2.50 for 100 bags of black or green tea, loose-leaf tea grown and processed in the United States can cost as much as $1 per gram. (It takes about 2.5 grams of loose-leaf tea to brew a single cup.) The sheer rarity of US-grown tea justifies the high price, according to the US League of Tea Growers.

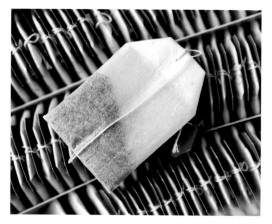

The most basic imported tea bag in the United States costs pennies, compared to at least a couple of dollars per serving for tea grown domestically.

The History of the Tea Bag

Who invented the first tea bag is the source of some debate. Roberta C. Lawson and Mary Molaren filed a patent for a "tea leaf holder" in 1901, describing it as a bag filled with enough leaves to brew a single cup of tea. The patented design was for a bag made from a stitched mesh fabric that was porous enough to let water flow through so tea could be infused. American tea importer Thomas Sullivan has also been credited with the invention. Sullivan started providing samples of his product in silk pouches around 1908. The small sachets weren't intended to be submerged in boiling water, but customers, not realizing this, used the bags to steep their tea, and the concept caught on.

Original tea bags were handmade, often stitched from muslin or silk. Commercial production of tea bags dates back to the 1920s. The design was so effective that few tweaks have been made in generations—even major tea manufacturers like Lipton and Twinings embraced porous teabags that allow water to flow through, releasing the tea flavor. The most significant innovation in tea-bag design involved adding strings with decorated tags to make it easier to remove the tea bag from the cup or pot when the tea was steeped.

CHAPTER 2
CHOOSING PLANTS FOR YOUR TEA GARDEN

This chapter is dedicated to all of the diverse plants you can use to brew tea, divided into five categories: classic tea, leaves, flowers, fruits, and roots. There is no one-size-fits-all tea garden and no list of plants that "should" be included, so don't be afraid to get creative. Choose plants based on their flavors or health benefits or aesthetic appeal; experiment with new plants; remove plants that aren't working for you. Fill your tea garden with plants you love, and enjoy sipping and sharing your garden-to-teacup brews.

Tea (Camellia sinensis)

All tea comes from one species of evergreen shrub.

All types of true tea—white, green, black, and oolong—come from one evergreen shrub plant: *Camellia sinensis*. Although the leaves and buds of all varieties of *Camellia sinensis* can be used to make tea, two varieties are most common: *C. sinensis* var. *sinensis* and *C. sinensis* var. *assamica*. It is the processing of the harvested plant that determines which of the four types of tea will be produced (more on this in the individual descriptions of each type of tea that follow).

Native to China, *C. sinensis* var. *sinensis* is most often used to make white, green, and oolong teas. The plant has smaller leaves

What Plant Hardiness Zone Do I Live In?

The US Department of Agriculture (USDA) established a Plant Hardiness Zone Map to help gardeners determine which plants would grow best in their locations. The map divides the nation into thirteen distinct growing zones, with each zone subdivided into "a" and "b" categories, based on average minimum winter temperatures. In the coldest zone, zone 1a, which includes Alaska, minimum winter temperatures range from -60°F to -55°F (-51°C to -48°C); in zone 13b, the island of Puerto Rico, average minimum winter temperatures range from 65°F to 70°F (18°C to 21°C). Cultivate outdoor plants that suit your zone, or cultivate other plants indoors or in a greenhouse. You will find a reproduction of this zone map on pages 136–139.

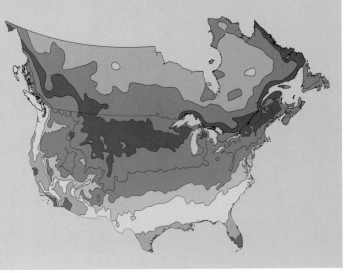

and favors drier, cooler climates, making it ideal for higher elevations. *C. sinensis* var. *assamica* hails from India and is the preferred variety for producing black tea. The large-leafed plant thrives in subtropical climates and areas with warm, humid climates. Some cultivars have variegated leaves ('Variegata'), pink flowers ('Rosea'), or twisted stems ('Contorta').

The evergreen shrubs have been cultivated in their native Southeast Asia for thousands of years; the tea plant is so ubiquitous that plants have been found growing wild across the continent. In the United States, tea can be grown in USDA hardiness zones 7 to 9 (and overwintered in greenhouses or high tunnels in cooler climates). It's also possible to grow tea plants in pots; use a camellia/azalea soil mix.

Plant *Camellia sinensis* in spring or fall. You can source plants from retail or online garden centers; you can also grow tea from seeds or rooted cuttings. To grow new plants from seed, harvest seeds, plant them, and tend them, and new plants will sprout in the garden.

Camellia sinensis grows up to 15 feet (4.6m) tall and 10 feet (3.1m) wide and produces white flowers between October and December. It prefers part shade. Choose a location where plants are protected from strong winds. It grows best in acidic soil with a pH of 6.5 or lower. Control the size and shape of the plants by pruning branches after flowering.

Growing tea requires patience. It takes about three years before *Camellia sinensis* leaves can be harvested. Once the plants reach maturity, pick young shoots with two to three leaves and use them to make white, green, black, or oolong tea. Different processing creates the different types of tea—read on for more details.

Did you know that tea plants produce flowers?

When harvesting tea leaves, pick only young shoots of two to three leaves.

WHITE TEA

White tea is the least processed type of tea. Made with the soft, unopened leaf bud on the tip of each stem, white tea—named for the white color of the buds—is the sweetest and mildest tea. Harvest in early spring when the buds are still closed.

Wither: Spread the buds out on a tray in a warm, humid area with good circulation and leave them out for a few hours. This process is called withering because the leaves dry out and start to look and feel withered.

Dry: Put the buds in the oven at 120°F (50°C) for twenty minutes, shifting them several times. You can also dry the buds in a food dehydrator, but the higher temperatures can have a negative impact on the flavor.

Sip: Add 1 teaspoon (5ml) of buds to hot—but not boiling—water and let steep for two to three minutes. Strain the buds before sipping.

White tea is made with the unopened leaf buds rather than opened leaves.

GREEN TEA

Green tea is made from the tender, light green leaves that appear in the spring. Though green tea is not a highly processed form of tea, it still undergoes a specific process between plant and cup. Harvest the top two leaves and the leaf bud from the plant and follow these steps.

Steam: Insert a steamer into a saucepan filled with ½ inch (1.5cm) of water, cover, and let it boil. Once the water reaches a rolling boil, add the leaves and cover again, steaming the leaves for two minutes. This stops the leaves from oxidizing and releases the fresh, just-picked flavor in the leaves.

Cool: Remove the pan and run the leaves under cold water.

Roll: Roll the leaves between your palms to shape them. There is no correct shape; turn them into small balls or tubes. The goal is to make tight shapes so that it's easier to dry the leaves. Working the leaves into tight balls or tubes releases the moisture, turning the leaves brown.

Dry: Spread the rolled leaves on a baking dish and put them into a preheated oven at 230°F (110°C) for ten minutes. The leaves should become dry and brittle.

Sip: Add 1 teaspoon (5ml) of buds to a cup of boiling water and let steep for three to five minutes. Strain the buds before sipping.

Green tea leaves can be used immediately after undergoing the drying process or stored in an airtight container for future use. Brewed green tea will be green to yellow in color and mildly astringent.

Here is what a handful of rolled tea leaves looks like.

The youngest spring leaves are harvested for green tea.

Don't forget to strain!

Matcha

This traditional tea originated in China and was once the preferred beverage of Buddhist monks and samurai warriors. Matcha, which means "ground tea," has become wildly popular in the United States thanks to its vibrant green color and health benefits. It's made from shade-grown green tea leaves. The best *Camellia sinensis* for matcha are said to be Japanese varieties *amidori*, *okumidori*, and *yabukita*. The leaves are harvested once per year, dried, and then de-stemmed and de-veined before being ground into a fine powder. The process is so labor intensive and specialized (hence the high cost of matcha) that it's not recommended as a DIY endeavor.

BLACK TEA

Black tea is made from oxidized leaves of the *Camellia sinensis* var. *assamica* plant. During oxidation, oxygen causes the tea leaves to turn dark brown to black, giving black tea its signature bold, rich flavor. To make black tea, pick the leaf bud and top two leaves on the plant and follow these steps.

Wither: Place the fresh leaves on a screen (to allow airflow) and leave them out for at least twenty-four hours.

Roll: Roll the leaves between your palms to shape them. Working the leaves into tight balls or tubes releases the moisture, turning the leaves brown.

Oxidize: Spread the leaves out on a baking dish in a single layer. Leave them out to be exposed to oxygen. Room temperature, around 70°F (21°C), is ideal. Leave them out for two or more hours until the leaves turn brown.

Dry: Place the oxidized leaves in an oven preheated to 245°F (118°C) for fifteen to twenty minutes. The leaves should become brittle.

Sip: Add 1 teaspoon (5ml) of buds to a cup of boiling water and let steep for three to five minutes. DIY black tea is much weaker than commercial brews, so you might need a longer steep time than you're used to. Strain the buds before sipping.

Remember that home-harvested black tea needs to be steeped longer than store-bought black tea.

OOLONG TEA

Oolong tea falls between black tea and green tea. How close it is to either depends on the tea master; some are more or less oxidized than others before the leaves are rolled. The steps to make oolong tea are similar to the steps used to make green and black tea. Pick the leaf bud and top two leaves on the plant and follow these steps.

Wither: Place fresh leaves on a screen and leave them out until the leaves start to turn brown.

Roll: Roll the leaves between your palms to shape them. Working the leaves into tight balls or tubes releases the moisture, turning the leaves brown.

Oxidize: Spread the leaves out on a baking dish in a single layer. Leave them out to be exposed to oxygen. Room temperature, around 70°F (21°C), is ideal. For tea with a lighter flavor that is closer to green tea, let them oxidize for up to ten hours; for a bolder flavor that is closer to black tea, let the leaves wither for twenty-four hours.

Dry: Place the oxidized leaves in an oven preheated to 245°F (118°C) for fifteen to twenty minutes. The leaves should become brittle.

Sip: Add 1 teaspoon (5ml) of leaves to a cup of boiling water and let steep for one to three minutes. Strain the leaves before sipping.

Oolong isn't as well known as black or green tea, but it is certainly worth trying.

Leaves

ANISE HYSSOP
(*Agastache foeniculum*)
■ **Zones**: 4 to 8

This herbaceous perennial bursts into bloom from June to September. Its tight spikes of lavender to purple flowers provide nectar that attracts butterflies and hummingbirds, earning it the nickname "hummingbird mint." In a tea garden, its foliage is the main attraction. As its name suggests, anise hyssop produces fragrant leaves with a strong anise (licorice) flavor.

Native Americans prized anise hyssop for its medicinal uses. Thanks to its antibacterial and anti-inflammatory properties, the herb, also known as blue giant, has been used to relieve congestion, reduce fevers, ease coughing, and alleviate diarrhea.

The light green, heart-shaped leaves can be plucked straight from the plant and added fresh to boiling water for a refreshing, flavorful tea; the dried leaves and flowers can also be used to make both hot and iced tea.

Anise hyssop is native to North America and grows well in sun to part shade. Although it tolerates most soil conditions, it requires good drainage to thrive. The clumping perennial grows up to 4 feet (1.2m) tall and 1 to 3 feet (30 to 90cm) wide. A member of the mint family, anise hyssop spreads via rhizomes and will aggressively self-seed; consider planting it in containers to keep it from taking over the garden.

☕ For the best brew:

Add 2 teaspoons (10ml) of fresh anise hyssop leaves or 1 teaspoon (5ml) of dried leaves to 1 cup (240ml) of boiling water. Let steep for five minutes; strain the leaves before sipping.

APPLE MINT
(*Mentha suaveolens*)
■ **Zones**: 5 to 9

Apple mint is a fast-growing ground cover with rounded leaves. Thanks to the fine hairs covering its leaves, apple mint earned the nickname "woolly mint." Despite being part of the mint family, apple mint has a fruity fragrance and a hint of apple flavor; it's less minty than other kinds of mint.

An aggressive spreader, apple mint grows up to 2 feet (60cm) tall and just as wide. Pruning the rhizomes helps control the spread; planting apple mint in pots will also keep it from taking over the garden. Choose a location in full sun to part shade and keep the soil moist. Cut the flower spikes after the pink or white flowers bloom in July and August to stimulate new growth.

Pineapple mint (*Mentha suaveolens* 'Variegata') is a subspecies of apple mint and has variegated foliage that makes it distinct from other mint species. The leaves have a strong fragrance and sweet citrus-mint flavor. To maintain the attractive green-and-white leaves, prune all of the pure green leaves, which will take over if allowed. White or light pink flowers blossom in July and August, attracting pollinating insects. Like its parent plant, pineapple mint grows up to 2 feet (60cm) tall and prefers full sun to part shade and moist soil. It's also a vigorous spreader.

Both apple and pineapple mint contain vitamins A and C, calcium, iron, and potassium. Both are used for ailments ranging from indigestion to headaches. Tea can be served hot or iced. Other mints, like spearmint or peppermint, or fruit-flavored herbs, like pineapple sage, complement the flavors of both apple mint and pineapple mint tea.

☕ For the best brew:

Add 1 cup (240ml) of apple (or pineapple) mint leaves or ½ cup (120ml) of dried leaves to 2 cups (480ml) of boiling water. Let steep for thirty minutes and strain the leaves before serving. For iced tea, follow the same directions but let the water cool overnight before straining and serve over ice.

BEARBERRY
(*Arctostaphylos uva-ursi*)
■ **Zones**: 2 to 7

Though bearberry gets its name for the clusters of berries that attract hungry bears, in a tea garden, this evergreen shrub is prized for its leaves, stems, and roots, not its fruit.

Native to northern regions in the United States, Canada, Europe, and Asia, bearberry is hardy enough to survive severe winters and will struggle in hot and humid climates. In the right climate, though, bearberry

is easy to grow. Plant it in full sun and acidic, well-drained soil. Once established, bearberry is drought tolerant. A mature shrub will grow just 1 foot (30cm) high and spread up to 6 feet (1.8m) wide. The white to light pink flowers bloom in April and May, and fruits start ripening in August.

Bearberry is also known as *kinnikinnick*, an Algonquin word that means "smoking mixture" and alludes to Native American tribes using the dried leaves in pipes. It also has a long history of use as a medicinal plant that is believed to protect the immune system, alleviate headaches, reduce inflammation, and prevent urinary tract infections. Bearberry might induce labor and should not be used during pregnancy; in large doses, it can also cause symptoms such as nausea, vomiting, fever, and chills.

The fruits lack flavor, but the leaves, which have a strong, earthy flavor, can be used fresh or dried in tea. It's often called uva ursi tea.

☕ *For the best brew:*

Add 2 teaspoons (10ml) of dried bearberry leaves to 2 cups (480ml) of boiling water; steep for at least fifteen minutes. Strain the leaves before sipping. To make iced tea, steep 2 teaspoons (10ml) of dried bearberry leaves in 2 cups (480ml) of boiling water; steep overnight. Strain the leaves and pour over ice.

BEE BALM
(*Monarda fistulosa*)
■ **Zones**: 3 to 9

Bee balm, also known as wild bergamot, is popular in pollinator gardens because pollinators like bees and butterflies like the nectar-rich flowers. The fragrant perennial herb, a member of the mint family, produces clusters of pom-pom-like flowers atop square stems. Bee balm blooms from July to September.

The Oswego Indians used bee balm in teas, so the earliest versions of the herbal teas were called Oswego tea. Different kinds of bee balm have different flavors. The leaves of scarlet bee balm (*Monarda didyma*) have a light citrus flavor; lavender bee balm has a stronger flavor that is most similar to bergamot orange. Although bee balm smells like Earl Grey tea and was even used as a replacement for black tea after the Boston Tea Party, the essential oil used in the iconic tea is from a different plant. The leaves of bee balm make amazing citrus-flavored tea and can be used fresh or dried.

Bee balm grows well in sun to part shade and well-drained soil. Like other mints, bee balm can be aggressive. In the garden, divide the plant in the fall to keep growth in check or plant it in containers to keep it from taking over—but be sure that the containers are large enough. Bee balm starts out small but grows to 2 to 4 feet (60cm to 1.2m) tall and can spread up to 3 feet (90cm). The plant is prone to powdery mildew; any leaves that show the telltale signs—circular white spots on the leaves, yellowing, and wilting—should not be used in tea.

The herb is a natural source of thymol, an antiseptic used in mouthwash. Oil from the leaves has been used for a range of ailments from respiratory infections and fevers to stomachaches, headaches, and insomnia.

⬛ For the best brew:

Add 2 tablespoons (30ml) of fresh bee balm leaves or 1 tablespoon (15ml) of dried leaves to 1 cup (240ml) of boiling water. Let steep for ten minutes; strain the leaves before sipping.

BLACKBERRY
(*Rubus* sp.)

- **Zones**: 6 to 8

Blackberries, plucked straight from the vine, are one of the highlights of summer. To make great tea, though, look to the leaves. Although the flavor is mild (and a little sweet), the leaves contain antioxidants, vitamin C, and tannins.

The bushes, available in erect or trailing and thorny or thornless varieties, are great fruit-bearing plants for beginning gardeners. The easy-to-grow plants grow best in full sun and acidic, moist—but not wet—soil. Trailing blackberries, such as 'Olallie,' need a

trellis for support. Blackberries self-pollinate, which means that you don't need multiple bushes for fruit production.

The erect, thornless cultivar 'Navaho' produces an abundance of mature fruit in July. 'Illini Hardy' also produces fruit in July; the erect and thorny cultivar is winter hardy and thrives in colder climates.

Mature blackberries are firm and black in color. Harvest them in the morning or evening, when temperatures are cooler, and refrigerate your take after picking. You can use both fresh and dried leaves in tea. Fermenting the leaves brings out their flavor. To ferment, crush wilted leaves, wrap them in a damp cloth, and store them in a warm, dark area for seventy-two hours. Remove the leaves from the cloth and dry them before brewing.

Thanks to their high antioxidant content, blackberries are known for lowering cholesterol and reducing the risk of cardiovascular disease; the berries are also high in vitamin C, calcium, potassium, and magnesium.

🍵 *For the best brew:*

Add 1 teaspoon (5ml) of fermented blackberry leaves to 2 cups (480ml) of boiling water and steep for three to five minutes. Strain the leaves before sipping.

CARDAMOM
(*Elettaria cardamomum*)
■ **Zones**: 10 to 13

Cardamom, often called Queen of the Spices, is one of the most expensive spices in the world. The tropical plant is labor-intensive to grow; the small seed pods used to produce the prized spice are slow to ripen and can take years to mature. After harvesting, the pods must be washed and dried. Green cardamom (so-called for the color of the pods) is harvested before the pods mature and has a sweeter flavor; black cardamom is dried and has its seeds extracted, resulting in a more pungent flavor. Cardamom gives chai its distinctive flavor.

Cardamom is native to tropical and subtropical climates like India, Sri Lanka, and Indonesia. In most of North America (zones 9 and lower), cardamom must be grown indoors or in greenhouses. The plants, which can grow up to 10 feet (3.1m) tall, do not tolerate drought. Choose a location with a lot of filtered sunlight and a lot of space to spread out.

Cineole, one of the essential oils in cardamom, is a potent antiseptic hailed for killing bacteria and banishing bad breath, making the pods popular breath fresheners. Research has also found that cardamom improves glucose intolerance, reduces inflammation, and helps prevent weight gain.

Cardamom pairs well with other strong, aromatic flavors, including cloves, cinnamon, and allspice. Because cardamom is a member of the ginger family, using it with the pungent root creates a can't-miss flavor combination.

🍵 For the best brew:

Add 1 teaspoon (5ml) of ground cardamom to 2 cups (480ml) of hot, not boiling, water. Steep for five minutes. Strain the cardamom before drinking.

CATNIP
(*Nepeta cataria*)
■ **Zones**: 3 to 7

Cats go wild for this intoxicating herb. Although it gives felines a natural high, the perennial is known for its calming effect in humans.

Catnip contains nepetalactone, the active ingredient in the herbal sedative valerian, so it's used to tame anxiety, insomnia, and nervousness, and it boosts mood. Its sedative effects can cause drowsiness, so brew tea in the evening, not first thing in the morning, and avoid drinking catnip tea and driving. Catnip is also effective for indigestion, stomach cramps, and gas. The herb might stimulate uterine contractions and trigger menstruation, so pregnant women and those with menstrual disorders, such as pelvic inflammatory disease, should not use catnip.

The perennial is native to Europe and parts of Asia but has adapted well to the United States. It grows up to 3 feet (90cm) tall and just as wide. In cooler climates, you can plant catnip in full sun, but opt for part shade in areas where it's hot and humid because those conditions can cause its demise. Catnip is drought-tolerant and prefers drier soils.

Pollinators are drawn to the flowers, which are white with pale purple markings and bloom from spring through fall. After the flowers bloom, snip the flower spikes to encourage a second bloom period. Plant catnip in containers because this member of the mint family is a vigorous spreader.

The fragrant gray-green leaves have a mild mint flavor with a hint of citrus (adding a lemony herb like lemon verbena or lemon balm enhances the citrus flavor). Catnip can be used fresh or dried.

Catmint (*Nepeta mussinii*) can also be used for tea. The plants are similar, but catmint, with its showier purple flowers, is more ornamental than catnip; different kinds of catmint have less aggressive growth habits.

☕ *For the best brew:*

Add 1 tablespoon (15ml) of dried catnip or 2 tablespoons (30ml) of fresh catnip leaves to 1 cup (240ml) of boiling water and let steep for at least ten minutes. Add a squeeze of lemon to bring out the citrus flavor.

CHICKWEED
(*Cerastium arvense*)

■ **Zones**: 3 to 8

This plant thrives in open spaces such as lawns and pastures, leading it to be considered more of a noxious weed than a flavorful herb. The perennial spreads via rhizomes and taproots, which cause it to form dense mats that can spread up to 3 feet (90cm) wide. Delicate white flowers bloom from April to August.

Multiple kinds of chickweed can be found worldwide. Field chickweed (*C. arvense*) is native to North America. Common chickweed (*Stellaria media*) and mouse-ear chickweed (*C. fontanum*) are native to Europe and now grow across the United States. All species have earned a reputation as weeds and are often killed with herbicides.

Most chickweed prefers cooler climates and often pops up in alpine areas, thriving beneath tree canopies. In areas where summer temperatures are sweltering, chickweed struggles to survive. The herb grows best in full sun and drier soils; too much moisture can cause root rot.

Harvest chickweed to appreciate its fresh flavor, which is often compared to that of corn silks. Chickweed contains beta-carotene, calcium, magnesium, potassium, selenium, and vitamin C. It's used for digestion, constipation, asthma, inflammation, and muscle and joint pain. The leaves, stems, flowers, and seeds can all be eaten raw or cooked.

For the best brew:

Add 2 tablespoons (30ml) of fresh chickweed or 1 tablespoon (15ml) of dried chickweed to 1 cup (240ml) of boiling water and steep for at least five minutes. Strain the greens before drinking.

CHOCOLATE MINT
(*Mentha* × *piperita* 'Chocolate')
■ **Zones**: 5 to 9

Despite its name, this perennial herb doesn't taste like chocolate. Instead, chocolate mint has a strong peppermint flavor similar to the mint flavor in peppermint patties—though some people claim that it's possible to detect subtle chocolate notes.

Chocolate mint is a cultivar of peppermint. Although the perennial herb, like other kinds of mint, is good for headaches, digestion, and fevers, its real benefit is its culinary uses. Adding chocolate mint to black tea gives it a hit of peppermint; the dark green to purplish leaves are also great on their own, fresh or dried, in a cup of mint tea. The cool menthol flavor is also excellent in hot chocolate and baked goods.

Like all herbs in the mint family, chocolate mint spreads rapidly. Pinching back the leaves will keep it from going to seed, and regular division can prevent its aggressive spread. Although chocolate mint is smaller than other mints, expect it to grow 2 feet (60cm) tall and 2 feet (60cm) wide.

You can start new plants from cuttings. Grow chocolate mint in containers to keep it from taking over the garden, and move the containers indoors to overwinter in a sunny window. Chocolate mint prefers full sun but will tolerate part shade; keep soil moist and harvest the leaves before the plant flowers.

🍵 *For the best brew:*

Add 1 cup (240ml) of fresh chocolate mint leaves or ½ cup (120ml) of dried leaves to 1 cup (240ml) of boiling water. Let steep for ten minutes and strain the leaves before serving.

CILANTRO/CORIANDER
(*Coriandrum sativum*)
- **Zones**: 2 to 11

Cilantro, typically called coriander in the United Kingdom, might seem like an odd addition to a tea garden, but the annual herb has a complex flavor that's been described as fresh and citrus-like (though some people have a genetic trait that makes it taste like soap to them). It's a unique plant that produces two distinct spices: the leaves are

sold as cilantro, and the seeds, which ripen in small, round pods, are sold as coriander. The leaves on the bottom of the plant are broader and more parsley-like, while the newer leaves at the top of the plant are more delicate. Mature seeds also have a hint of citrus and, when roasted, a nuttier flavor. Both the leaves and the seeds are used in teas.

Cilantro produces seasonal flowers in white, pink, and pale purple, and it grows up to 2 feet (60cm) tall. It's considered a cool-weather annual. In hot climates, cilantro is known to bolt, a process that leads plants to go to seed and die. To keep cilantro from bolting, either pinch off the flowers or plant in late summer, after the hottest part of the season, and harvest in fall.

Cilantro grows well in gardens or containers. For the herb to thrive, plant it in well-drained soil and part shade. Beware of planting in full sun; if the heat is too intense, cilantro could succumb to sunscald.

Both the leaves and the seeds of this herb are chock full of nutrients. Cilantro (the leaves) contains vitamins A and K, folate, potassium, manganese, and beta-carotene; coriander (the seeds) has several minerals, including calcium, magnesium, and potassium. The herb is believed to combat bacterial infections, ease digestive upset, lower blood sugar, improve sleep, and protect against colon cancer.

🫖 For the best brew:

Add 1 tablespoon (15ml) of fresh cilantro leaves or ½ tablespoon (7.5ml) of dried leaves to 1 cup (240ml) of boiling water. Let steep for five minutes and strain leaves before serving.

EUCALYPTUS
(*Eucalyptus perriniana*)
- **Zones**: 8 to 10

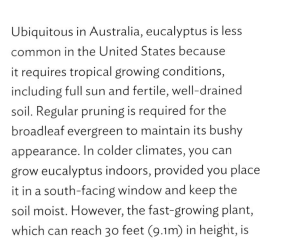

Ubiquitous in Australia, eucalyptus is less common in the United States because it requires tropical growing conditions, including full sun and fertile, well-drained soil. Regular pruning is required for the broadleaf evergreen to maintain its bushy appearance. In colder climates, you can grow eucalyptus indoors, provided you place it in a south-facing window and keep the soil moist. However, the fast-growing plant, which can reach 30 feet (9.1m) in height, is apt to outgrow its pot too quickly to make it a popular houseplant. A cold snap can kill eucalyptus.

Despite the challenges of growing eucalyptus, the health benefits associated with the tropical plant make it a worthwhile endeavor. The oil from the gray-green leaves of the eucalyptus tree has antimicrobial and antibacterial properties that can help ease colds, sore throats, bronchitis, and respiratory problems. Research has also found eucalyptus to be an effective pain reliever, easing pain associated with joint strains, arthritis, and backaches.

Eucalyptus tea is made from ground leaves. Thanks to the sweet menthol flavor, eucalyptus has a cooling sensation, though the flavor is often described as bitter. Crushing the leaves helps release the flavor. Ginger is a good flavor complement.

For the best brew:

Add 1 tablespoon (15ml) of crushed, fresh eucalyptus leaves to 2 cups (480ml) of boiling water and let steep for up to ten minutes (steep for less time to reduce the bitterness). Strain the leaves before drinking.

FENNEL
(*Foeniculum vulgare*)
- **Zones**: 4 to 9

In the Middle Ages, hanging fennel over doors was believed to keep out evil spirits. Today, the herb is prized for its medicinal uses. Fennel is used for digestion, gastrointestinal distress, appetite regulation, metabolism, hypertension, congestion, and menstrual cramps. The herb is antibacterial, antifungal, and anti-inflammatory.

You can grow fennel as a perennial herb or an annual bulb. As an herb, fennel is a perennial that produces green foliage and seeds used in herbal medicine. The bulb (*F. vulgare* var. *azoricum*) is also known as

anise fennel because of its amazing licorice flavor. You can plant bulbs in spring and fall, providing two annual harvests.

The bulbous base, thick stocks, and feathered fronds make fennel look like a cross between two of its relatives: celery and dill. Clusters of small yellow flowers appear on the ends of short stalks, creating the appearance of a flat flower head. The bloom period ends in July, and seeds replace the flowers. Harvest just as the flowers start to fade. Clip the stems with the flower heads and hang them in a dark spot until dried.

Grow fennel in full sun and moist soil, where it will grow up to 6 feet (1.8m) tall and 3 feet (90cm) wide. To keep fennel from self-seeding and taking over the garden, remove the flowering stems before seeds appear.

Fennel is a larval plant for certain swallowtail butterflies; bees also love the flowers. The licorice flavor makes fennel popular as a culinary herb that is eaten raw, dried, stewed, or grilled. When making tea, adding fennel seeds to boiling water can destroy the nutrients.

🍵 For the best brew:

Boil 2 cups (480ml) of water and let it rest for three minutes. Add 2 teaspoons (10ml) of fresh fennel seeds or 1 teaspoon (5ml) of dried fennel seeds to the water and let steep for ten minutes. Strain the seeds before serving.

HOLY BASIL
(*Ocimum sanctum*)
■ **Zones**: 2 to 11

The significance of this "holy" herb is as impressive as its flavor. Holy basil was said to be growing around Christ's tomb after the resurrection and, in some Greek Orthodox churches, it's used to prepare holy water. In India, the tender perennial is called *tulsi*, which means "the incomparable one."

Different varieties of holy basil have different flavors. Rama is the most common and has lighter green leaves and a stronger, more clove-like taste; Vana, which often grows wild, is the most fragrant and has notes of licorice; and Krishna, with its dark green, almost purple, leaves, has a stronger, peppery flavor. All varieties of tulsi are more aromatic and sweeter than traditional Italian basil and can be a sweet complement to tart flavors like ginger, cinnamon, and turmeric. It's known for alleviating digestive upset, relieving stress, and calming colds.

Holy basil, native to Africa and Asia, grows best in hot temperatures and drier soil (if basil is watered too often, it will rot). It blooms from June to first frost. Although the herb is sensitive to frost, it's possible to place root cuttings in water and overwinter the rooted plants in a sunny window. The flavor is at its peak when the leaves just start to bud, but leaves can also be dried and used in tea blends.

🍵 *For the best brew:*

Add 4 tablespoons (60ml) of fresh holy basil leaves or 2 tablespoons (30ml) of dried leaves to 4 cups (960ml) of boiling water. Let steep for fifteen minutes and strain leaves before serving.

LAVENDER MINT
(*Mentha × piperita* 'Lavender')
■ **Zones**: 5 to 9

Lavender mint, as its name suggests, has a rich lavender flavor and floral scent. The leaves have light purple undersides, and the flowers, which bloom from June to September, are both lavender in color and scent.

Like all mints, lavender mint is fast growing, prefers full sun to part shade, and likes moist, well-drained soil. It grows up to 2 feet (60cm) tall and spreads 2 feet (60cm) (or more) wide. It's a red-stemmed mint (like peppermint) and is often used dried, but fresh lavender mint can be used in teas, too.

Both the leaves and the flowers can be used in tea. Combine lavender mint with lavender for a tea that is floral in both flavor and fragrance; lemon herbs also complement the flavor.

For the best brew:

Add ¼ cup (60ml) of fresh lavender mint leaves or 2 tablespoons (30ml) of dried lavender mint to 1 cup (240ml) of boiling water and let steep for ten minutes. Strain the leaves before drinking.

LEMON BALM
(*Melissa officinalis*)

■ **Zones**: 3 to 7

The name is a little misleading. While this perennial herb has a lemon scent and citrus flavor, lemon balm is actually a member of the mint family. The flavor is best described

as light; recipes featuring lemon balm as an ingredient often call for lemon juice, too, because the herb is too mild to pack a lemony punch. Even with a handful of fresh leaves, a cup of lemon balm tea will still only have a mild, minty flavor.

Lemon balm spreads like other mint species, making it best confined to a container where it won't take over the garden. The low-growing herb grows about 18 inches (45cm) high and is often used as ground cover. Bees love the white and yellow flowers that bloom from June to August; in fact, the herb was once called bee balm. Plant it in full sun and water it often; regular pruning during the growing season helps keep it from going to seed or spreading too fast.

As a medicinal herb, lemon balm is used to reduce stress and anxiety and promote sleep. It loses much of its flavor after it's dried, so lemon balm is best brewed from fresh leaves. To make dried herbal teas with lemon balm, be careful not to bruise the leaves during harvesting, and hang the cuttings in a moisture-free environment so the stems don't rot.

🍵 For the best brew:

Add 1 tablespoon (15ml) of fresh lemon balm or ½ tablespoon (7.5ml) of dried lemon balm to 1 cup (240ml) of boiling water. Let steep for fifteen minutes and strain leaves before serving.

LEMONGRASS
(*Cymbopogon citratus*)

■ **Zones**: 8 to 11

A tender perennial that looks like clumps of tall grass, lemongrass is best known as a fragrant addition to Asian dishes. It's native to India and Sri Lanka and prized around the globe for its health benefits, which range from easing sore throats and reducing inflammation to aiding in digestion and alleviating headaches.

Lemongrass grows wild in tropical grasslands. In warmer climates in the United States, the clumping grass requires more attention. Lemongrass, an evergreen in zones 10 and higher, grows up to 4 feet (1.2m) tall and 3 feet (90cm) wide and performs best in full sun. You can also plant it in containers and grow it indoors.

For the best flavor, harvest lemongrass when the stalks are firm, green on the top, and light yellow on the bottom; avoid leaves with brown edges. Store fresh lemongrass in the refrigerator or freezer or cut it into pieces and dry it.

Lemongrass has bright green foliage with a powerful scent that makes it a common ingredient in perfume and soap. The flavor is strong, too. As its name suggests, lemongrass has a zesty citrus flavor; you can use it fresh or dried without sacrificing flavor. Lemongrass blends well with mint, bay leaves, and ginger.

The leaves are sharp and inedible. You must mash the grass with a mortar and pestle or put it through a food grinder; even then, the blades can still be sharp, so it's essential to strain the tea well to avoid swallowing any pieces of the plant.

🍵 *For the best brew*:

Add three stalks of fresh lemongrass to 3 cups (720ml) of water. Bring the water to a boil; cover and let simmer for fifteen minutes. Strain the lemongrass before drinking.

LEMON VERBENA
(*Aloysia citriodora*)
■ **Zones**: 8 to 10

This deciduous shrub, also known as lemon beebrush, lemon luisa, and Yerba Louisa, is native to South America. Lemon verbena can grow up to 15 feet (4.6m) tall. The narrow leaves grow in groups of three around the stems, and clusters of small white to lavender flowers bloom in the summer and fall.

The leaves have such a powerful citrus scent that lemon verbena is often considered the strongest of the lemon-scented plants. Lemon verbena wasn't just named for its scent; the lemon flavor is intense, too. In fact, the leaves are often used as a substitute for lemon zest in recipes. Both the leaves and flowers, fresh or dried, are used in teas. The flavor is best when the leaves are fresh; dried lemon verbena has a milder flavor, but, even when it's subtle, the lemon is unmistakable. The flavor in the leaves is strongest during flowering. It only takes a small number of leaves to brew a strong cup of lemon tea.

Lemon verbena is said to be good for relieving heartburn and indigestion; it's also said to be a sedative that helps alleviate insomnia and anxiety.

Plant lemon verbena in light shade and moist, well-drained soil, and prune the leaves throughout the growing season to maintain its shape. This low-maintenance herb can be overwintered indoors in a bright but cool spot.

☕ For the best brew:

Add ½ cup (120ml) of fresh lemon verbena leaves or ¼ cup (60ml) of dried leaves to 2 cups (480ml) of boiling water. Let steep for at least ten minutes and strain the leaves before serving.

MARJORAM
(*Origanum majorana*)

■ **Zones**: 9 to 10

A relative of oregano, this Mediterranean herb has a milder, more delicate flavor. It's grown as a tender perennial in warmer climates; further north, marjoram grows well as an annual.

The aromatic and flavorful gray-green leaves make marjoram a popular culinary herb that is often used in stews, roasts, and stuffing; the leaves can also be steeped to make tea. As a medicinal herb, marjoram is believed to be beneficial for treating cold and flu symptoms such as runny nose, cough, and infection. It is also used for digestive issues, migraines, and nerve pain, though studies on its effectiveness are limited. Small studies have shown that marjoram improves cardiovascular health by reducing blood pressure and improving blood flow.

Marjoram prefers full sun and neutral or alkaline soils with a lot of sandy loam; a low-maintenance plant, it tolerates heat and drought. The low-growing plants can get up to 2 feet (60cm) tall and produce white to pale pink flowers during the summer months. Harvest marjoram before it flowers, when the flavor of the leaves is at its peak. Cutting the stems before the plant flowers will also make the plant bushier. Use marjoram leaves fresh or dried.

⬛ *For the best brew:*

Mix 1 teaspoon (5ml) of fresh marjoram leaves or ½ teaspoon (2.5ml) of dried marjoram with 1 cup (240ml) of boiling water and let steep for three to five minutes. Strain the leaves before serving.

PARSLEY
(*Petroselinum crispum*)
■ **Zones**: 2 to 11

Parsley has been relegated to the side of the plate for too long. Often used as a garnish, parsley is both delicious and nutritious. The Mediterranean herb is high in vitamins A and C and minerals like potassium, iron, and copper. It has been used to prevent kidney stones, relieve joint pain, and combat anemia; parsley has also been declared an anticancer powerhouse, thanks to studies that show it combats free radicals, prevents cell damage that can lead to cancer, and inhibits tumor growth. Parsley is known to increase menstrual flow and should not be used by pregnant women.

This annual grows in full sun to part shade and moist, well-drained soil. It prefers cooler climates and can wilt in hot, humid summers. Avoid growing parsley from seed because it has a long germination period. It's possible to overwinter herbs indoors in a bright window.

Parsley has a light, fresh flavor with a hint of bitterness. Curly parsley (var. *crispum*) and Italian parsley (var. *neapolitanum*) are among the most common varieties of the popular herb. Although Italian parsley has a stronger flavor, the varieties can be used interchangeably. You can use all parts of the plant—leaves, seeds, and roots—in teas; make parsley tea with fresh or dried herbs.

🍵 For the best brew:

Add 2 tablespoons (30ml) of fresh or dried parsley leaves to 1 cup (240ml) of water. Steep for two to three minutes. Parsley loses its flavor when it's exposed to heat for long periods of time, so keep the steep time to a minimum.

PATCHOULI
(*Pogostemon cablin*)
- **Zones**: 8 to 12

Perhaps best known as an essential oil used in beauty products, patchouli is also a powerful medicinal herb that has been used to treat health conditions such as depression, inflammation, stress, fever, and insomnia—but too much patchouli can make insomnia worse and might trigger a loss of appetite and nervousness. The distinctive scent has earned it the nickname "stinkweed."

Patchouli is native to Southeast Asia and grows best in hot, humid climates. In colder

regions, patchouli should be considered an annual. It prefers part shade and fertile, well-drained soil. It might not seem obvious from its aroma, but patchouli is a member of the mint family and is known as a fast-growing herb that can spread up to 3 feet (90cm) wide. Like other mints, patchouli grows well in containers and can be moved indoors for overwintering. The herb is prone to pests, such as caterpillars, and diseases, such as leaf blight.

P. cablin grows up to 3 feet (90cm) tall and produces large, oval leaves with deep veins; small white flowers appear in the fall and have no discernable fragrance. Another species, *P. heyneanus*, sometimes called Java patchouli, has a similar growth habit and produces light purple-pink flowers. Pluck leaves in the morning when their oils are strongest.

The taste of patchouli, like the fragrance, is not universally appreciated. To make patchouli tea more palatable, pair it with basil, bergamot, lavender, rose, and other herbs often blended with patchouli in perfumes and other scented products.

For the best brew:

Add 1 teaspoon (5ml) of dried patchouli leaves to 2 cups (480ml) of boiling water and steep for three to five minutes. Strain the leaves before sipping. Add honey to taste.

PEPPERMINT
(*Mentha × piperita*)

■ **Zones**: 5 to 9

Peppermint might be mistaken as a species all its own, but it was developed by crossing watermint (*Mentha aquatica*) and spearmint (*Mentha spicata*). The result is an herbaceous perennial with robust mint flavor and fragrance. The leaves from fresh peppermint plants have a stronger flavor than dried leaves, but both are strong enough to make a delicious cup of tea.

The hybrid mint isn't just a popular herbal tea ingredient; peppermint is also known as a powerful medicinal herb that is used to soothe upset stomachs and aid in digestion; its numbing effect also makes it effective for treating headaches, depression, and anxiety.

Peppermint grows in full sun to part shade and tolerates high temperatures as long as it's watered often and the soil is kept moist. Since it's a hybrid, peppermint is sterile and cannot be grown from seed; root it from cuttings instead.

Pretty pink flowers bloom in July and August—remove them after bloom to stimulate new growth. The plant, which grows up to 2 feet (60cm) high and 2 feet (60cm) wide, grows aggressively. Peppermint's rapid spread has earned it a spot on the USDA's invasive species list. Plant it in containers to keep it from taking over the garden.

🍵 *For the best brew:*

Add ½ cup (120ml) of fresh peppermint leaves or ¼ cup (60ml) of dried leaves to 2 cups (480ml) of boiling water. Let steep for at least ten minutes and strain the leaves before serving.

PINEAPPLE SAGE
(*Salvia elegans*)
■ **Zones**: 8 to 11

Hummingbirds and butterflies love pineapple sage's pretty tubular, scarlet flowers, which bloom between August and October, while tea drinkers appreciate the citrus flavor and scent that earned it its moniker.

The tender perennial is native to Mexico and Central America, where it grows as a small, clumping shrub that reaches up to 4 feet (1.2m) high and 3 feet (90cm) wide. In zones 7 and lower, you can grow pineapple sage as an annual that will survive until the first frost; alternatively, you can grow it in pots and overwinter it indoors. Pineapple sage grows best in full sun and well-drained soil.

Despite its name, pineapple sage has no relation to the pineapple plant or the sage plant. It's a member of the same Lamiaceae family as mint. Like other mints, it eases upset stomachs and aids in digestion; pineapple sage might be calming (some studies show it has mild antidepressant effects), and it is often used to treat sleep disorders.

Pineapple sage is a mild herb. Crush the leaves to release the fragrance and tangy citrus flavor. The red flowers are edible, too, and taste like citrus and mint. Make teas from fresh or dried leaves and flowers.

☕ *For the best brew:*

Add ½ cup (120ml) of pineapple sage leaves to 1 quart (960ml) of boiling water; let steep for fifteen minutes or longer to maximize the delicate flavors.

ROSEMARY
(*Rosmarinus officinalis*)
■ **Zones**: 8 to 10

One of the most popular culinary herbs, rosemary is native to the Mediterranean and often paired with heartier fare, such as lamb, pork, and potatoes. It's prized for the strong aroma of its thin, needle-like gray-green leaves and its robust flavor, which is best described as minty with light pine notes—not surprising, given that it's a woody herb.

Grow this perennial shrub in full sun and acidic soil. In colder climates, you can overwinter rosemary indoors, provided it receives enough sunlight (or artificial light). Don't overwater rosemary; it prefers drier soil. If it's overwatered, the plants will develop root rot. Pruning plants after the white flowers bloom in June or July helps encourage denser foliage growth. If left to grow wild, rosemary will get lanky.

Rather than stripping the leaves from the stems to make tea, steep the entire sprig to achieve the best flavor. Young stems have the strongest flavor, but older stems (and dried rosemary) also produce great-tasting tea. You can also turn rosemary into a powder. To do this, remove the leaves from the stem and then place ¼ cup (60ml) of rosemary in the microwave for two to three minutes (or until the leaves start to crumble when touched). Use a mortar and pestle to crumble the leaves into a powder.

Rosemary is hailed as a natural health powerhouse that aids in digestion, enhances cognitive function, reduces inflammation, and improves liver function. It is also known to cause side effects, ranging from nausea and vomiting to uterine contractions; pregnant women should avoid drinking rosemary tea.

🍵 *For the best brew:*

Add 1 teaspoon (5ml) of fresh, dried, or powdered rosemary to 1 cup (240ml) of boiling water and let steep for five minutes. Strain the leaves before drinking the tea.

SAGE
(*Salvia officinalis*)
- **Zones**: 4 to 8

Though sage grows well in cooler climates, the herb is native to the Mediterranean and northern Africa, where it has a long record of medicinal use. Native Americans also used sage in their healing rituals. Research shows that sage can be effective for easing sore throats, lowering cholesterol, improving mood, and protecting against neurological disorders, such as dementia. Thanks to a compound called thujone found in some of the 900-plus kinds of sage, too much of the herb might cause restlessness, vomiting, rapid heart rate, vertigo, or seizures.

The easy-to-grow perennial herb produces oblong gray-green leaves on woody stems. It grows like a small shrub, reaching 2½ feet (75cm) tall and wide. In June, sage blooms with light purple to blue flowers. The tubular blooms, which can reach up to 1 inch (2.5cm) in length, grow on upright stalks, and their nectar attracts bees and butterflies. Grow sage in full sun and let the soil dry out between watering. If the soil is too wet, sage can succumb to root rot.

Sage has fragrant leaves and an astringent flavor that has been described as a cross between citrus and eucalyptus; it's sweet with a hint of bitterness and pairs well with dairy, savory foods, and beer. In tea, sage pairs well with other citrusy flavors, including lemon verbena, lemon balm, and pineapple sage. Sage can be used fresh or dried.

🫖 *For the best brew:*

Add 2 tablespoons (30ml) of fresh sage leaves or 1 tablespoon (15ml) of dried sage to 1 cup (240ml) of boiling water and let steep for at least five minutes. Strain the leaves before drinking.

SPEARMINT
(*Mentha spicata*)
■ **Zones**: 5 to 9

Spearmint is one of the more delicate mints. Its sweet flavor is a natural complement to other sweet ingredients, including lavender and chamomile, but the herb also works well with savory spices such as cinnamon and winter savory (*Satureja hortensis*), another member of the mint family.

The perennial ground cover prefers sun or part shade and medium to wet soil. It grows

up to 2 feet (60cm) tall and 2 feet (60cm) wide and produces delicate white, light pink, or lavender flowers that attract butterflies during their summertime bloom. Each type of spearmint has large, toothed leaves, but 'Kentucky Colonel' mint—the cultivar preferred for mint juleps and mojitos—has larger (and arguably more attractive) leaves.

Clip spearmint after it blooms to promote growth. The herb grows rapidly, so you will need to divide it seasonally; plant it in pots to keep it from spreading where it's not wanted. While you can harvest spearmint throughout the season, the leaves become bitter after the plant flowers, so for the best flavors, harvest before blooms appear. The flavors are best when leaves are fresh, not dried.

Spearmint has been shown to manage inflammation, boost the immune system, and alleviate digestive upset. It's not recommended for pregnant women because it could damage the uterus; excessive consumption could also cause kidney damage.

☕ *For the best brew:*

Add ½ cup (120ml) of fresh spearmint leaves or ¼ cup (60ml) of dried leaves to 2 cups (480ml) of boiling water. Let steep for at least ten minutes and strain the leaves before serving.

STINGING NETTLE
(*Urtica dioica*)

■ **Zones**: 3 to 10

Stinging nettle is a staple in herbal medicine. Its leaves are excellent sources of vitamins A, C, and K; several B vitamins; beta-carotene; calcium; copper; iron; magnesium; and potassium. The perennial herb is used for allergies, muscle aches, urinary tract infections, and inflammatory diseases

such as osteoarthritis and gout. However, it can stimulate uterine contractions and shouldn't be used when pregnant. Despite its nutritional value and healing properties, stinging nettle isn't a popular garden plant. The herb is often used as a stand-in for spinach because it has a bitter flavor.

The fast-growing plant is often considered an invasive weed. It grows wild under forest canopies, alongside streams, and in pastures, where it thrives because the stems and undersides of the leaves are covered in small hairs (trichomes) that wildlife avoid. The trichomes release histamine-based fluids when broken. (The genus name *Urtica* comes from a Latin word that means "to burn," and it was so named for the burning sensation it causes when the trichomes penetrate the skin.)

Stinging nettle prefers full sun and damp, rich soil. In ideal conditions, stinging nettle can grow up to 4 feet (1.2m) tall. A distant cousin to mint, stinging nettle is also fast spreading and, if left unchecked, will take over the garden. Grow it in containers and prune often, or harvest in the wild (in areas not sprayed with pesticides).

The small hairs are sharp, so it's best to wear gloves, long pants, and long sleeves when planting and harvesting stinging nettle. Choose a spot in the garden that pets and children cannot access to prevent them from coming in contact with the prickly plants.

For the best brew:

Add 2 tablespoons (30ml) of dried nettle leaves to 4 cups (960ml) of water. To preserve the vitamin content, heat the water until it's hot but not boiling. Steep for thirty minutes and strain the leaves before drinking.

ST. JOHN'S WORT
(*Hypericum calycinum*)
■ **Zones**: 5 to 9

This popular medicinal herb is perhaps best known as a natural antidepressant. Researchers believe that hypericin, a natural chemical compound in the plant, helps improve mood by acting on neurotransmitters in the brain. St. John's wort also contains hyperforin, a powerful reuptake inhibitor of brain chemicals such as serotonin and dopamine that play a role in depression. It's believed to be as effective in treating mild to moderate depression as prescription medication.

In addition to its mood-boosting benefits, St. John's wort is also used to treat wounds and alleviate hot flashes during menopause. It's such a potent medicinal herb that France has banned products made with St. John's wort because of potential interactions with some medications. There are also concerns that it might contribute to dementia in those diagnosed with Alzheimer's disease, worsen symptoms of attention deficit hyperactivity disorder, trigger mania in those with bipolar disorder or psychosis in those with schizophrenia, and impair fertility. For these reasons, use this herb with great caution.

St. John's wort is an easy-to-grow deciduous shrub native to Southern Europe and Asia. Grow it as a ground cover—its maximum height is 18 inches (45cm)—in full sun to part shade. It prefers well-drained, sandy soil. Root rot is common in hot, humid climates.

Large yellow flowers that resemble roses bloom in July and August. Cut back leaves in late winter or early spring to promote vigorous new growth. St. John's wort grows rapidly, spreading via underground stems, and is considered an invasive plant in some areas of the United States because it chokes out native plants. Keep growth in check by planting the herb in containers. The herb is also toxic to livestock and shouldn't be planted in or around pastures.

Both the leaves and flowers can be used in tea. The flowers have a light lemon flavor; the leaves are earthier and more pungent.

For the best brew:

Steep 3 teaspoons (15ml) of fresh leaves or flowers in 1 cup (240ml) of boiling water and let steep for four minutes. Strain the herb before drinking.

THYME
(*Thymus vulgaris*)
- **Zones**: 5 to 9

Thyme is a small plant with mighty flavor. The small, oval, blue-green leaves have a flavor that has been described as a cross between mint, citrus, and pine; thyme has a strong mint fragrance. For the best flavor, harvest the aromatic leaves right before the plants flower.

This annual ground cover, known as garden thyme or common thyme, pairs well with other types of thyme, including lemon thyme (*Thymus × citriodorus*) and other mint species.

Native to Europe and parts of Asia and Africa, thyme grows up to 15 inches (38cm) tall and remains evergreen in warmer climates. Bees and butterflies love the pale purple flowers that bloom from May to July.

Thyme is considered a low-maintenance annual that tolerates drought and nutrient-poor soils; if the soil gets too wet, the herb could get root rot. Plant thyme in full sun and trim the stems as needed to prevent them from getting too woody.

Both fresh and dried thyme is associated with health benefits such as relieving menstrual cramps, easing indigestion, aiding sleep, and preventing infections. Thymol, the active ingredient, is an antioxidant. Ingesting too much thyme can cause vomiting and nausea, and thyme isn't recommended for pregnant women because of the risk of miscarriage.

🫖 For the best brew:

Add 2 teaspoons (10ml) of fresh or dried thyme leaves to 1 cup (240ml) of boiling water. Let steep for at least ten minutes.

WITCH HAZEL
(*Hamamelis virginiana*)
- **Zones**: 3 to 8

Witch hazel is both ornamental and medicinal. The shrub is a showstopper during the fall, when the leaves turn brilliant shades of gold and flowers with petals that look like thin yellow ribbons emerge. The fragrant flowers bloom between October and December, often clinging to the branches long after the leaves drop. Seeds appear after the flowers die and provide an important food source for wildlife.

The low-maintenance deciduous shrub grows up to 20 feet (6.1m) tall. Witch hazel will grow in partial shade, but the blooms are better if it's planted in full sun and moist, acidic soil. *H. virginiana* is the only witch hazel that blooms in the fall; vernal species (such as *H. vernalis*) bloom in the spring.

Both the leaves and bark are used in topical treatments to soothe sensitive skin. As a medicinal herb, witch hazel treats inflammation, sore throats, colds, and the flu. The leaves and bark can be used in tea.

🍵 *For the best brew:*

Use a sharp knife to strip small patches of bark from the tree before the leaves emerge in the spring. Cut the bark into small pieces and add 1 cup (240ml) of fresh bark or ½ cup (120ml) of dried bark to 2 cups (480ml) of boiling water. Let steep for forty-five minutes. To make tea from witch hazel leaves, add 1 tablespoon (15ml) of fresh leaves or ½ tablespoon (7.5ml) of dried leaves to 1 cup (240ml) of boiling water and let steep for twenty minutes. Strain the bark or leaves before sipping.

YAUPON
(*Ilex vomitoria*)
■ **Zones**: 7 to 9

Yaupon is a broadleaf evergreen that is believed to be the only plant native to North America that contains caffeine. Research shows that the 'Nana' cultivar has as much caffeine as green tea; adding nitrogen fertilizer can increase caffeine content up to 265 percent. Yaupon is a member of the holly family, and some kinds of holly are poisonous, so be sure to only make tea from *Ilex vomitoria*.

Native Americans drank yaupon tea as a ceremonial drink. While yaupon fell out of favor as both a tea and a medicinal plant, Native Americans continued to grow the shrub as an ornamental. It grows up to 20 feet (6.1m) tall and 12 feet (3.7m) wide and has glossy green leaves that provide color year round. Grow yaupon in full sun to part shade and moist soil. Both a male and female plant are required to bear small red berries that ripen in late fall. Birds love the berries, but the fruit isn't required to make tea.

Yaupon has about the same levels of antioxidants as blueberries. The tea is used to control blood pressure, aid digestion, ease constipation, reduce inflammation, and boost the immune system. It's not recommended for those with heart issues or women who are pregnant.

Yaupon tea is more complicated to brew than herbal infusions because the leaves need to be roasted first. It has a slight bitterness and is similar in flavor to green tea.

For the best brew:

Place a thin layer of freshly harvested yaupon leaves on a baking sheet and place them in the oven, preheated to 350°F (177°C), until the leaves start to turn brown (about fifteen minutes). Once the leaves cool, use a mortar and pestle to crumble them finely. Add 1 tablespoon (15ml) of dried leaves to 1 cup (240ml) of water. Bring the water to a boil, stir in the leaves, and let simmer for at least five minutes. The longer it steeps, the stronger the flavor will be. Strain the leaves before drinking. Store excess tea in a sealed jar.

Flowers

CALENDULA
(*Calendula officinalis*)

■ **Zones**: 2 to 11

The brightly colored flowers and long bloom times make calendula popular garden annuals. Different types of calendula, also known as pot marigold, produce single and double daisy-like flowers in a range of hues from light yellow to deep orange. The color—and the plant's popularity as a dye—earned calendula the nickname "poor man's saffron."

Calendula blooms from May through August; removing dead flowers can encourage subsequent blooms. The annual, which can survive as a perennial in zones 8 and higher, prefers cooler climates. Grow in full sun—part shade in warmer climates—and well-drained soil. Calendula can grow 1 foot (30cm) tall and 2 feet (60cm) wide. Cutting back the plants will encourage bushier growth.

Cultivated around the world for medicinal use, calendula is both anti-inflammatory and antimicrobial. It's used to calm upset stomachs, alleviate heartburn and acid reflux, ease sore throats, and combat respiratory infections. Calendula can stimulate menstruation, so pregnant women shouldn't consume it.

Add color to dishes like soups and salads with fresh flower petals. The edible flowers have flavors ranging from bitter to peppery. Calendula pairs well with rose hips (*Rosa rugosa*), safflower (*Carthamus tinctorius*), and all kinds of mint. Though you can dry calendula petals, the flavor is best in fresh flowers.

🍵 For the best brew:

Harvest 2 tablespoons (30ml) of fresh or dried calendula flowers and add to 1 cup (240ml) of boiling water. Steep for fifteen minutes and strain the flowers before drinking.

CHAMOMILE
(*Matricaria recutita*)
■ **Zones**: 2 to 8

Chamomile might be the most popular herbal tea. It's made from the daisy-like flowers of the German chamomile plant. The flowers, with yellow centers and white petals, bloom from June through August. Dried flower heads are used to make chamomile tea. (The stems smell great but are too bitter to use in tea.)

The word *chamomile* is of Greek origin and means "apple on the ground." The herb was named for its apple-like aroma and flavor. With mild sedative properties that aid in relaxation, the soothing herbal tea is often the plants grow up to 2 feet (60cm) tall. For optimal growth, do not overwater. Chamomile will tolerate poor soils. Although it's considered an annual, chamomile might self-seed and return to the garden for subsequent seasons. Plants are easy to grow from seed.

Roman chamomile (*Chamaemelum nobile*) is a more petite species of chamomile. Although it's slightly more bitter and less sweet than German chamomile, it still makes flavorful herbal tea.

recommended as a sleep aid. Chamomile tea also helps with colds and flu, headaches, and stomach upset. Citrus-flavored herbs such as lemon balm and lemon verbena are great complements to chamomile.

German chamomile, also known as sweet false chamomile, is as ornamental as it is flavorful. Native to Western Europe,

For the best brew:

Add 1 tablespoon (15ml) of dried chamomile flowers to 1 cup (240ml) of boiling water. Steep for at least five minutes; strain the flowers before sipping.

DANDELION
(*Taraxacum officinale*)

■ **Zones**: 2 to 10

Dandelions are among the first signs of spring, their bright yellow flower heads popping up among blades of grass, between cracks in the sidewalk, and along roadsides.

 These "weeds" are a staple of Chinese medicine, and tinctures made from the roots, leaves, and flowers are used to make restorative tonics. Dandelions contain vitamin C, fiber, potassium, beta-carotene, and protein. They are used to help with digestion and liver function and to fight off colds and the flu. All parts of the plant are also used in salads, wine, and tea.

Dandelions aren't typically cultivated in the garden so much as killed for having the nerve to push through the soil. Rather than purchasing the perennial herb at garden centers or ordering seeds through seed catalogs or online, dandelions are best harvested in the wild. Look for places off the beaten path that likely have not been sprayed with chemical weed killers. Eating dandelion greens has become so mainstream that some upscale supermarkets, including Whole Foods, stock them in the produce department.

Unlike the leaves, which have a bitter flavor, the flowers are sweet. (Younger leaves are less bitter than more established leaves.) The roots, once dried and roasted, are often used to make a coffee-like drink. To roast the roots, harvest and wash them well, cut them into pieces, place them on parchment paper, and put them in the oven at 200°F (93°C). Roast until the roots snap easily; this might take several hours. Cool and store in a sealed jar. To use, grind the roots and add them to coffee grounds at a 1:1 ratio.

You can use all parts of the dandelion, fresh or dried. Since the flowers and leaves have different tastes, use them as separate herbs rather than adding both to a single brew. Consider adding sweeter herbs, like mint or lemon balm, to dandelion tea to offset the bitterness in the leaves. Serve dandelion tea hot or iced.

🍵 *For the best brew:*

For dandelion flower tea, separate the dandelion petals from the base of the flower. Pour boiling water over ½ cup (120ml) of dandelion petals and let steep for twenty minutes. (The flowers have a delicate flavor that requires a longer steep time to appreciate.) For dandelion leaf tea, add 4 tablespoons (60ml) of dandelion leaves to 1 cup (240ml) of boiling water and let steep for five minutes; add sweetener to taste.

ECHINACEA
(*Echinacea purpurea*)
■ **Zones**: 3 to 9

A staple in herbal medicine, echinacea is revered for its ability to fight infections, including colds and the flu. This perennial contains vitamins A, B, and E as well as minerals, including calcium and iron. All parts of the plant—leaves, flowers, and roots—are used in both herbal medicine and tea.

Echinacea is actually a genus, but it is used as a common noun to refer to several different species, which are also referred to as coneflowers. *E. purpurea*, native to the eastern United States, is called purple coneflower. Yellow coneflower (*E. paradoxa*) is native to Arkansas, Missouri, Oklahoma, and Texas and produces yellow flowers. Tennessee coneflower (*E. tennesseensis*) is, as its name suggests, native to Tennessee, and it also produces purple blooms.

Coneflowers are as pretty as they are practical. *E. purpurea* is a perennial that produces flowers with daisy-like purple petals radiating from prominent conical orange centers that bloom from June to August. If you don't remove the flowers, the seed heads will blacken and attract birds in search of a nutritious meal; the nectar-rich flowers are favorites of bees and butterflies. Japanese beetles also love echinacea and make fast work of defoliating the plants. Leaving seed heads intact allows for vigorous self-seeding.

Grow echinacea in full sun to part shade and well-drained soil. This heat- and drought-tolerant herb grows well in poor soil. Echinacea will grow up to 5 feet (1.5m) tall. The colorful blooms make excellent cut flowers.

☕ *For the best brew:*

Add 1 teaspoon (5ml) of fresh flowers, leaves, or roots (chopped) or 2 teaspoons (10ml) of dried plant material to 2 cups (480ml) of boiling water. Let the brew steep for at least five minutes and strain before drinking.

HIBISCUS
(*Hibiscus rosa-sinensis*)
- **Zones**: 9 to 11

The bright blooms on these tropical beauties command attention. Chinese hibiscus is one of a number of hibiscus varieties grown for their evergreen leaves and saucer-sized flowers. The single or double blossoms can reach up to 8 inches (20cm) in diameter and come in shades ranging from white, light pink, and apricot to red and orange. Hibiscus flowers often last just one day, so pluck them immediately to use in tea.

Chinese hibiscus, also called China rose, rose mallow, and Hawaiian hibiscus, grows up to 10 feet (3.1m) tall. Below zone 10, hibiscus needs to be overwintered indoors. Other species, such as *H. lasiocarpos*, will survive the winters in colder climates.

Plant in full sun to part shade and in a location protected from strong winds; keep soil moist. Chinese hibiscus is sensitive to changes in its environment. Shifts in temperature, humidity, light, and soil moisture can cause leaves to yellow or drop.

Tea brewed with the antioxidant-rich flowers and leaves has been shown to lower blood pressure, increase HDL (aka "good") cholesterol, and fight infections, such as bronchitis. Some studies have also found that drinking hibiscus tea aids weight loss.

The flowers turn water a lovely pink hue that makes hibiscus tea feel like a festive brew. Hibiscus tea has a tart flavor; cut it with lemon or lime juice. Adding honey also adds sweetness. Prepare hibiscus tea hot or iced.

For the best brew:

Add 1 cup (240ml) of fresh hibiscus flowers or ½ cup (120ml) of dried flowers to 10 cups (2.4 liters) of boiling water and let steep for five minutes. Strain the flowers before sipping. Add sweetener to taste. For iced tea, follow the same process but allow the water to cool. Serve over ice.

JASMINE
(*Jasminum officinale*)
- **Zones**: 7 to 10

making traditional jasmine tea. Jasmine prefers full sun to part shade and can grow up to 15 feet (4.6m) wide and twice as tall. The fast-growing vine needs a trellis or other support. A profusion of fragrant blooms appears from April to September. Jasmine should be pruned after flowering to control its rapid growth. Pollinators love the nectar-rich, tubular flowers that are white to pale pink.

The deciduous vine has been associated with health benefits, such as lowering cholesterol, reducing the risk of heart attack, improving the immune system, easing inflammation, and preventing diabetes. Because jasmine is acidic, drinking too much jasmine tea may cause stomach upset.

Jasmine tea has been around since 1300 AD. The fragrant and flavorful tea is so time consuming to prepare that it was once reserved for royalty. Tea leaves and jasmine flowers are harvested at different times, so, in traditional preparation, tea leaves were harvested and stored until the jasmine flowers bloomed, and then the fresh flowers were layered with green tea until the leaves absorbed the perfume from the flowers. Some of the most prized varieties of jasmine tea repeat the process multiple times for a tea that has a floral flavor and heady scent.

Growing the vine is much easier than

For the best brew:

In a glass jar, add ½ cup (120ml) of fresh jasmine flowers to 1 cup (240ml) of dried loose-leaf green tea, sandwiching the green tea between layers of flowers. Seal the jar, let it sit for at least twenty-four hours, and then shake the jar to mix the flowers and tea leaves. To brew, add 1 teaspoon (5ml) of this jasmine tea mix to 1 cup (240ml) of boiling water and let steep for at least five minutes. Strain the tea before serving.

LAVENDER
(*Lavandula angustifolia*)

■ **Zones**: 5 to 8

Although Provence is famous for its colorful fields of lavender, the fragrant perennial is not native to France. Despite it being commonly called English lavender, it's not native to England, either. Lavender hails from the Mediterranean. (French lavender, *Lavandula dentata*, is also from the Mediterranean.)

Lavender is an herbaceous perennial that grows in upright clumps. Long shoots of purple flowers bloom atop narrow gray-green leaves. It's best suited to full sun and well-drained soil, but it will tolerate poor soil and drought. Keep stems from turning woody by aggressively pruning plants after bloom; thin annually.

🍵 *For the best brew:*

Mix 2 tablespoons (30ml) of fresh lavender flowers or 1 tablespoon (15ml) of dried flowers to 2 cups (480ml) of boiling water. Let the tea steep for at least five minutes and strain the flowers before drinking.

There are several different cultivars of English lavender. 'Hidcote' is known for its dark purple flower spikes; it has a fruitier flavor than other kinds of lavender. 'Lavenite Petite' hails from New Zealand and produces pom-pom-like flower spikes. 'Miss Katherine' is one of few pink types of lavender and has elegant sprays of deep pink blooms. All lavender species can be used in tea.

Lavender is prized for its fragrance, making it a popular ingredient in soaps, bath oils, and perfumes. Thanks to the healing effects of its essential oils, the plant has a long history of use in folk medicine for a range of ailments, including insomnia, depression, chronic pain, muscle spasms, digestion, inflammation, and stress. Too much lavender can trigger side effects like nausea and vomiting.

Lavender is related to both mint and rosemary; the taste is often described as a marriage of those flavors. While the flavor is pleasing to most, some perceive the taste as soapy. With its spicy floral flavor—with hints of mint and lemon—lavender is excellent when paired with chamomile, lemon-flavored herbs, or bergamot, the orange-flavored herb that gives Earl Grey its distinctive flavor.

MILK THISTLE
(*Silybum marianum*)
■ **Zones**: 5 to 10

Milk thistle, also called blessed thistle, is an unusual-looking biennial that produces a bright pink-purple flower with spiked bracts that bloom in summer. The plant gets its name for the milky sap released when the tall stem and prickly leaves are cut.

Native to the Mediterranean region, milk thistle grows best in full sun and well-drained soil. The plants are prone to aggressive self-seeding and are considered invasive in some states. Remove spent flower heads after bloom to keep milk thistle from taking over the garden. Mature plants can grow up to 5 feet (1.5m) tall and 4 feet (1.2m) wide.

In addition to being a popular edible that is used in salads and soups, milk thistle is also known for its medicinal benefits. It's believed to bolster appetite, improve digestion and liver function, promote the production of breast milk, and protect against bone loss. Side effects can include headaches and stomach upset; it can also lower blood sugar levels, so those with diabetes should use it with caution. The use of milk thistle is believed to date back to 40 AD, when a Greek botanist used it to treat liver and gallbladder issues.

Each flower can produce up to 200 seeds per season. Milk thistle has a bitter flavor, so consider adding herbs with stronger flavors; mint and citrus are good options. Consider pairing with peppermint or lemon balm.

🫖 *For the best brew:*

Shake the seeds loose after the flowers bloom and crush them with a mortar and pestle. Add 1 tablespoon (15ml) of crushed seeds to 3 cups (720ml) of boiling water; steep for twenty minutes and strain the seeds before drinking the tea.

PURPLE PASSIONFLOWER
(*Passiflora incarnata*)

■ **Zones**: 5 to 9

Spanish conquistadors believed that the unusual-looking passionflower signified the Passion of Christ, the center of the flower being suggestive of the crown of thorns that Jesus wore during the crucifixion. Lore aside, passionflower is regarded as a powerful sedative, effective for treating insomnia, anxiety, attention deficit/hyperactivity disorder, and chronic pain. Those on antidepressants or antianxiety medications should not ingest passionflower.

There are more than 400 species in the genus *Passiflora*. *P. incarnata*, which is native to the eastern United States, is the hardiest of all passionflowers; other species, such as red passionflower (*P. coccinea*) and blue passionflower (*P. caerulea*), both native to Central and South America, require more tropical conditions to thrive and will do best in zones 9 and higher. The flowers, leaves, and stems of all species of passionflower can be used in teas.

Passionflower grows up to 8 feet (2.4m) tall and 6 feet (1.8m) wide; the vine will climb a support, like a trellis, if provided. Choose a location in full sun to part shade. The flowers have long, narrow, white petals with tricolored filaments in dark purple, lavender, and white; the centers have chartreuse stamens and purple stigmas. Passionflower blooms from July to September. The flowers have a mild, earthy flavor. Edible fruits, known as maypops for the popping sound they make when stepped on, appear in July; maypops can be eaten fresh from the vine or made into preserves.

The fast-growing vine spreads via root suckers and can take over a garden. Prune at the beginning of spring, cutting back stems to their base. Passionflower might not survive the winter in cold climates.

🍵 For the best brew:

Mix 1 tablespoon (15ml) of fresh passionflower leaves and flowers or 1 teaspoon (5ml) of dried leaves and flowers with 1 cup (240ml) of boiling water. Let steep for at least five minutes. The longer the tea steeps, the more complex the flavor becomes; it takes on a richer, almost toasted, flavor with a hint of bitterness.

RED CLOVER
(*Trifolium pratense*)

■ **Zones**: 3 to 10

Bees love these sweet perennial weeds that pop up in lawns in the spring. Red clover is a fast-growing ground cover with bright pink flowers that pop up like globes in the grass. Rather than breaking out the herbicides at the first sign of red clover, take a cue from the bees, who enjoy the flowers' sweet flavor.

Red clover also has myriad medicinal benefits. It is used to treat high cholesterol, respiratory infections, asthma, and indigestion, and to help prevent cancer. The flowers contain isoflavones that the body converts to phytoestrogens similar to estrogen, making red clover a popular herb to alleviate the symptoms of premenstrual syndrome and menopause, including hot flashes. Because red clover acts like estrogen, it should be avoided during pregnancy and breastfeeding.

The herbaceous perennials are ubiquitous in lawns, along roadsides, and in fields. They are widely considered weeds, so most garden centers don't sell red clover, but seeds are available. Beware that red clover can be aggressive; the stems send out nodules that creep through the grass, and a single plant can spread up to 12 inches (30cm). Planting it in containers and pruning it after it blooms will help control its spread. Plant in full sun to part shade; red clover blooms in May and June.

Farmers often use red clover and white clover (*T. repens*) for crop rotation because both are nitrogen fixers that add nitrogen back to the soil. When foraging for red clover, choose sites that haven't been sprayed with herbicides or pesticides.

🍵 For the best brew:

Add 2 tablespoons (30ml) of fresh flowers or 1 tablespoon (15ml) of dried flowers to 1 cup (240ml) of boiling water and let steep for ten minutes. Strain the flowers before drinking.

ROSE
(*Rosa* sp.)
- ■ **Zones**: 2 to 8

More than 100 species of rose belong to the genus *Rosa*. Roses, often cultivated for their beautiful flowers, come in a range of colors and fragrances; some roses climb, others trail, and most have thorns on their stems. Regardless of the species, the deciduous shrubs grow best in full sun and moist, well-drained soil. Late-winter pruning helps promote vigorous growth.

Roses can be temperamental. Most species are susceptible to a host of diseases and pest issues, including rust, powdery mildew, black spot, aphids, thrips, and mites. Implement organic controls if you will use rose petals in tea or edibles. Hybrid varieties, such as floribunda and grandiflora, are among the hardiest roses.

Unlike rose hip tea, which is made from the edible fruit of the rugosa rose (*Rosa rugosa*), rose tea is made from rose petals; both dried buds and fresh flowers make tea with a subtle floral fragrance and flavor. Rose tea, a popular hot beverage in the Middle East, can be intense. To tone it down, use fewer petals, add rose petals to green or black teas for rose-flavored tea, or mix flowers with other herbs, such as mint and chamomile.

Rose petals contain vitamins A and C, polyphenols, and antioxidants; tea made from the flowers is believed to ease menstrual cramps, improve digestion, relieve respiratory illnesses, promote sleep, boost mood, and stimulate the immune system.

For the best brew:

Add 1 cup (240ml) of fresh or dried rose petals to 3 cups (720ml) of boiling water. For rose-flavored black or green tea, add ¼ cup (60ml) of tea leaves to the brew. Let the tea steep for at least five minutes and strain the petals before drinking.

SKULLCAP
(*Scutellaria incana*)

■ **Zones**: 5 to 8

This native wildflower got its name for the skull-shaped calyx that covers the flower bud before it blooms. Thanks to the miniature white hairs, called hoary, covering its square stems, skullcap is often called hoary skullcap or downy skullcap. Skullcap produces small, tubular, purple-blue flowers from June to September that are attractive to pollinators.

Skullcap is native to the eastern United States, where it can be found growing wild in open woodlands and meadows and along stream banks, riverbanks, and ravines. The perennial grows up to 3 feet (90cm) tall and tolerates heat, drought, shade, and poor soils. A different variety, *Scutellaria lateriflora*, is also a native North American wildflower that produces blue flowers, hence its common name, blue skullcap.

As a medicinal plant, skullcap is believed to prevent inflammation and cause sedation, and it is often used for conditions ranging from insomnia and inflammation to high cholesterol and stroke. In high doses, it can cause confusion, twitching, irregular heartbeat, and seizures. Growing skullcap in the garden helps avoid commercial supplements that might contain germander (*Teucrium* sp.), a plant known to cause liver problems.

You can use fresh and dried flowers from the native plant in tea. Although skullcap is a member of the mint family, it has a slightly bitter, not minty, flavor. Adding 1 teaspoon (5ml) of fresh mint leaves to skullcap tea can help improve its taste.

☕ *For the best brew:*

Add 1 teaspoon (5ml) of fresh skullcap flowers or leaves to 2 cups (480ml) of boiling water and let it steep for three to five minutes. Strain the flowers before serving.

TRUMPET HONEYSUCKLE
(*Lonicera sempervirens*)
■ **Zones**: 4 to 9

Most of the 180 species of honeysuckle originated in Asia, but trumpet honeysuckle, not to be confused with trumpet vine, is native to the southeastern United States. The vines are vigorous growers, reaching 15 feet (4.6m) tall and 6 feet (1.8m) wide. If not supported by a trellis, the vines become dense ground cover.

Trumpet honeysuckle produces tubular scarlet flowers with orange and yellow insides in May and June. Nectar-seeking critters like birds, hummingbirds, and butterflies love the tubular flowers. While some honeysuckle has a heady scent, trumpet honeysuckle produces no discernible fragrance. The flowers have a delicate flavor. Pluck them after bloom for tea. The mild flavor almost disappears when the flowers are dried; use fresh flowers instead. Do not consume the red berries that appear in late summer and early fall.

The perennial vine, which is semi-deciduous in zones 8 and higher, should be pruned after bloom. Aggressive pruning can keep growth in check. Grow trumpet honeysuckle in full sun and moist, well-drained soil.

If you venture away from *Lonicera sempervirens*, be careful to choose the right species of honeysuckle for the garden. Both bush honeysuckle (*L. maackii*) and Japanese honeysuckle (*L. japonica*) are destructive invasive species that take over landscapes and choke out other plants.

All kinds of honeysuckle are known for their ability to reduce inflammation, ease upper respiratory infections such as colds and the flu, treat urinary tract infections, alleviate headaches, and help with digestive disorders. The pretty vine can also slow blood clotting and should be avoided before and after surgeries.

🍵 For the best brew:

Boiling water can cause honeysuckle flowers to taste bitter; use the flowers for iced tea to preserve their flavors. Gently crush fresh honeysuckle flowers to release their flavors and mix 1 cup (240ml) of flowers with 2 cups (480ml) of cold water. Stir and cover. Leave the mixture in the refrigerator overnight. Strain the flowers and pour over ice to serve.

TUFTED VIOLET
(*Viola cornuta*)
■ **Zones**: 6 to 11

The bloom of these petite flowers signals the arrival of spring. These tender perennials appear as early as March and remain in bloom throughout the summer, often flowering a second time in the fall. In hot climates, flowers might fade, but they can make a comeback in the fall. Plant in full sun or part shade.

Tufted violets are among 550 species in the *Viola* genus. Also known as pansies or Johnny jump-ups, violets are the state flowers for four U.S. states: Illinois, New Jersey, Rhode Island, and Wisconsin.

The tufted violet, also known as the horned violet, is a perennial that grows up to 8 inches (20cm) tall. Different varieties

🍵 *For the best brew:*

Add 2 tablespoons (30ml) of fresh or dried (chopped) leaves and flowers to 1 cup (240ml) of boiling water. Let the tea steep for ten minutes and strain before drinking.

produce different-colored flowers; most are two-toned in shades of blue, violet, lavender, yellow, orange, peach, and white (similar to pansies). The sweet violet (*Viola odorata*) is one of few tufted violets planted for its fragrance.

Research shows that violet leaves are chock full of vitamins. In fact, the leaves have as much vitamin C as an orange and similar vitamin A content to spinach. Harvest flowers and leaves throughout the season, but do not eat the roots; they can cause diarrhea. Use both fresh and dried leaves to make tea. Violets are used to treat a range of ailments, from headaches and congestion to sore throats and fevers.

YARROW
(*Achillea millefolium*)
■ **Zones**: 3 to 9

Pollinators love yarrow, which is also known by common names such as milfoil, bloodwort, and devil's nettle. In addition to attracting bees and butterflies, the fast-spreading, flowering ground cover also has a host of health benefits. A member of the aster family, yarrow fights bacteria and viruses; alleviates pain, including menstrual cramps and joint pain; and aids in digestion. The herb also triggers sweating, which can help reduce fevers.

Yarrow produces fern-like green leaves that spread into a tangled mass of foliage up to 3 feet (90cm) wide; left unchecked, it will take over the garden, giving it a reputation as an aggressive weed. The leaves are both aromatic and flavorful. Yarrow has a licorice-like aroma, but its leaves are sweet with a hint of bitterness. Small flowers in colors ranging from white and yellow to pink and red appear from June to September. Both flowers and leaves can be used in tea.

Plant yarrow in full sun and sandy soil; with good drainage, the perennial will tolerate poor soil and drought. If the soil is too moist, the stems will flop. High winds and rainstorms can also cause the plants to topple. When planted as a ground cover or turf replacement, yarrow can be mowed (on a high setting) to remain low growing.

☕ For the best brew:

Add 1 teaspoon (5ml) of dried yarrow flowers or 1 teaspoon (5ml) of dried yarrow leaves to 1 cup (240ml) of boiling water and steep for three to five minutes. Before drinking tea made from flowers or leaves, strain the herbs.

Fruits

BLACK CURRANT
(*Ribes nigrum*)

■ **Zones**: 3 to 7

Black currant is an underappreciated fruit. In spring, after the chartreuse flowers are spent, fruits appear. The bunches of green berries ripen to glossy black fruits starting in June. The flavor of black currants has been described as fresh and floral with notes of raspberries; the fruit is tart.

The berries are high in antioxidants, polyphenols, and gamma-linolenic acid, an omega-6 fatty acid that reduces inflammation. Black currants have four times more vitamin C than oranges and twice the antioxidants of blueberries. As a medicinal plant, black currant is used to boost the immune system, ease flu symptoms, and reduce joint and muscle pain and stiffness. Both fresh and dried berries and leaves can be used in hot or iced tea.

The compact bushes grow up to 4 feet (1.2m) tall and wide. It can take up to five years before the plants produce fruit. Black currant grows best in sun to part shade and moist, fertile soil. The self-fertile plants require regular pruning during the dormant season. Diseases and pests are an issue with black currants; plants are prone to gall mites, powdery mildew, and black currant leaf midge, which can affect growth and fruit production.

☕ For the best brew:

Add 2 teaspoons (10ml) of dried berries to 2 cups (480ml) of boiling water and steep for thirty minutes. The berries are safe to eat and can remain in the tea, or you can strain and set them aside. Alternatively, add 2 teaspoons (10ml) of fresh, chopped black currant leaves to 1 cup (240ml) of boiling water and steep for five minutes. Strain the leaves before sipping.

ENGLISH HAWTHORN
(*Crataegus laevigata*)

- **Zones**: 4 to 7

English hawthorn is native to Europe and North Africa. Its thorns made it a popular plant for hedgerows. The tree can grow up to 20 feet (6.1m) tall and is known for a profusion of flowers that appear in the spring; blooms range from white and pink to red, and some cultivars feature double flowers. Hawthorn produces small red fruit, sometimes called a haw, after the flowers

finish blooming. Birds love the fruit, so you might need to use netting to protect the harvest.

Hawthorn is known for its powerful antioxidants, called flavonoids, that are used to treat a range of heart-health issues, including high blood pressure, hardening of the arteries, irregular heartbeat, and congestive heart failure. As a result, hawthorn is often called the heart herb. The leaves, fruit, and flowers are all used in herbal medicine.

The non-native tree, also called midland or woodland hawthorn or simply mayflower, is better suited to cooler climates. In areas with hot, humid temperatures, hawthorn can succumb to diseases, such as fungal leaf spot and rust, that kill the foliage. The slow-growing tree thrives in full sun and moist, well-drained soil.

The fruit from the hawthorn tree is both sweet and sour. You can use it fresh or dried, and it pairs well with both florals and fruits; consider adding rose petals, hibiscus, or other berries to enhance the flavor.

☕ *For the best brew:*

Add 2 tablespoons (30ml) of dried hawthorn berries to 2 cups (480ml) of boiling water and steep for fifteen minutes. The berries are safe to eat and can remain in the tea, or you can set them aside to eat later.

PERSIMMON
(*Diospyros virginiana*)
■ **Zones**: 4 to 9

Though persimmons in the species *Diospyros kaki* are native to China, the fruits are also grown across the United States, including natively in the species *Diospyros virginiana*. In the spring, persimmon trees produce fragrant white to light green flowers; fruit appears in the fall. They're astringent before

they ripen, but when the small reddish-orange fruits are at their peak, they are sweet and have a pudding-like texture. (Ripe fruit is not too firm or too soft. Pressing the flesh should leave a light indentation.)

Persimmons have a flavor similar to apricots, but the fruit, which is less than 2 inches (5cm) in diameter, is not a stone fruit; persimmons are berries. Of the common cultivars, *Diospyros kaki* 'Hachiya' is more astringent and has a strong, tart flavor unless the fruit is ripe, while *D. kaki* 'Fuyu' produces a sweeter, tomato-shaped fruit.

Persimmons are not the best choice for a small garden. The trees grow up to 60

feet (18m) tall and need room to spread their branches. Most species are dioecious, which means that each tree is either male or female. Pollination—and fruit set—requires a male and female tree.

These colorful fruits contain vitamins A, C, and E; fiber; manganese; and copper. Persimmons also contain antioxidants that are beneficial for heart health and inflammation and might help lower LDL (aka "bad") cholesterol.

You can use both the leaves and the fruit (fresh or dried) from persimmon trees in hot or iced tea. The leaves have a mild, bittersweet flavor. Traditional brews are often blended with cinnamon, ginger, and turmeric.

☕ For the best brew:

To make persimmon tea from the fruit, slice two small persimmons, add to 10 cups (2.4 liters) of boiling water, and let simmer for twenty minutes. Add 1 tablespoon (15ml) each of grated turmeric root and ginger root for a pungent kick. Sweeten to taste. Another option is to add 1 tablespoon (15ml) of fresh, chopped leaves or ½ tablespoon (7.5ml) of dried leaves to 1 cup (240ml) of water and steep for several hours.

RASPBERRY
(*Rubus idaeus*)
■ **Zones**: 5 to 8

Raspberries are the perfect combination of sweet and tart. The delicate red fruits are part of a group of fruits called brambles that produce berries on canes. Most varieties produce white (and sometimes pink or light purple) flowers in April; berries ripen in the summer. It takes a full year before the plants produce fruit. Red raspberries are the most common, but other varieties produce fruits that are black, purple, and yellow.

Plant raspberries in full sun to part shade. The healthiest canes grow in well-drained, acidic soil. Wet soil can cause root rot. Raspberries are vigorous growers that reach 3 to 9 feet (90cm to 2.6m) tall and spread up to 3 feet (90cm) wide. Without pruning, raspberries can grow into impenetrable thickets. Canes that produce berries—called fruiting canes—need to be pruned to the ground after the fruit is harvested. In the spring, cut canes back again, removing about 25 percent of the canes. Watch for thorns.

Although raspberries are grown for their fruit, the bright green leaves are used in tea. Young leaves are the most flavorful. Harvest leaves in the spring before the fruit appears. Raspberry leaves taste like mild black tea. Both fresh and dried berries and leaves can be used in tea. If using berries, opt for iced tea.

For the best brew:

Add 2 tablespoons (30ml) of fresh raspberry leaves or 1 tablespoon (15ml) of dried raspberry leaves to 1 cup (240ml) of boiling water. Let tea steep for at least five minutes and strain the leaves before sipping. Fresh berries taste best in iced tea. Crush 1 cup (240ml) of fresh raspberries with ¼ cup (60ml) of sugar, add 1 teaspoon (5ml) of fresh mint leaves, and add to 2 cups (480ml) of boiling water; steep for fifteen minutes. Add the sweet raspberries to the tea made from fresh or dried raspberry leaves; steep for another five minutes.

RUGOSA ROSE
(*Rosa rugosa*)

■ **Zones**: 2 to 7

The rugosa rose produces edible fruits known as rose hips. Rose hips sit just below the petals and contain the seeds for the rose plant. These small fruits form in late summer, after the roses have bloomed, and are an excellent source of vitamin C, making them popular for treating colds and flu. Rose hips are also used to treat inflammation, high blood pressure, high cholesterol, fever, and stomach issues, including diarrhea and constipation. For health benefits, fresh rose hips are best because processing destroys the nutrients.

Rugosa rose is native to Asia. The deciduous shrub grows up to 6 feet (1.8m) tall and produces fragrant pink to white flowers; most have single petals, but some have semidouble or double petals. Without pruning, the rose throws out suckers and forms dense thickets. The stems are covered in sharp thorns. Like other species of rose, the rugosa rose is susceptible to several diseases, including black spot and powdery mildew, but is considered more disease resistant than most roses; disease resistance is improved when the roses are planted in full sun. Rugosa rose grows so well in coastal conditions, where it grows in sand dunes, that it has earned the nicknames "beach rose" and "salt spray rose."

You can make rose hip tea from both fresh and dried rose hips. It has a tart, fruity flavor.

🍵 *For the best brew:*

Pour 1 cup (240ml) of boiling water over ¼ cup (60ml) of fresh rose hips or 1 tablespoon (15ml) of dried rose hips. Let steep for fifteen minutes; strain the fruit before drinking.

STAGHORN SUMAC
(*Rhus typhina*)
- **Zones**: 3 to 8

Staghorn sumac, sometimes generally known as wild sumac, is best known for its bright red leaves and red berries that burst forth in the fall. The tree, which grows up to 25 feet (7.6m) tall, has rust-colored hairs covering its young branches, giving them a velvet-like texture. Leaves on the deciduous tree are bright green during spring and summer and transition to brilliant shades of red, orange, and yellow during the fall.

The berries on staghorn sumac, like the leaves, also have a fuzzy texture. The berries are juicy and have a tart citrus flavor, but, thanks to the texture, sumac berries are best spit out, not swallowed.

As its common name, wild sumac, suggests, staghorn sumac grows unbidden in woodlands and wetlands. It should not be confused with poison sumac (*Toxicodendron vernix*), a tree related to poison ivy and poison oak. Look at the berries to distinguish staghorn sumac from its poisonous relative: staghorn sumac has deep red berries growing on upright stalks, whereas the berries on poison sumac are white and hang from the branches. If you are not sure which species the berries come from, do not eat them.

The plant is popular in Middle Eastern and Mediterranean cooking. Thanks to high levels of antioxidants and vitamin C, Native Americans used sumac berries to treat colds, the flu, and scurvy. Research has shown that sumac berries help reduce blood sugar in those with type 2 diabetes.

🍵 For the best brew:

Pick several clusters of berries, crush them to release the flavor, and add them to 4 cups (960ml) of water to soak overnight. Strain the berries, add ice, and sip. You can also add sumac berries to boiling water, but the heat lowers the vitamin C content, so iced tea is more nutritious.

STRAWBERRY
(*Fragaria* × *ananassa*)

■ **Zones**: 4 to 9

It's believed that strawberries were so named because the plants are mulched with straw during the winter, but the exact origin of the name of these sweet berries is unknown. Described as one of America's most beloved fruits, strawberries are not fruits at all; the edible part of the plant is a receptacle of the flower.

Regardless of the botanical definition, strawberries taste wonderful eaten straight from the vine, baked, or brewed to make flavorful hot or iced tea. The plants are medicinal, too. Strawberries are helpful for stroke and heart disease prevention, blood pressure control, constipation, and blood sugar control; the fruits are chock full of vitamin C, fiber, folic acid, and potassium.

There are more than 600 kinds of strawberries. 'Honeoye' is a June-bearing strawberry that grows 6 inches (15cm) tall and spreads twice as wide when grown in full sun and fertile, moist soil. It produces petite white flowers with yellow centers that bloom in May and June, followed by a single crop of large, sweet berries.

Strawberries can succumb to a number of pests and diseases, making them difficult to grow. Leaf spot, root rot, leather rot, mites, aphids, and slugs are among the most common problems affecting the plants.

🍵 *For the best brew:*

To make iced tea, put ½ cup (120ml) of large, ripe strawberries in a food processor, blend until smooth, and strain the seeds. Boil 4 cups (960ml) of water and let cool. Once water is cool, add berries, steep overnight, and serve over ice. For hot tea, put ¼ cup (60ml) of fresh, ripe strawberries in 2 cups (480ml) of boiling water. Let steep for at least five minutes, strain the fruit, and serve.

Roots

BURDOCK
(*Arctium lappa*)
■ **Zones**: 3 to 7

Burdock root is a staple in Asian cooking, where it is often sautéed, braised, and served as a side dish. In the United States, it's often seen as a weed. The root of this exotic herb is packed with antioxidants, increases circulation, alleviates skin conditions like acne and psoriasis, and might inhibit tumor growth. In animal studies, burdock root appears to have aphrodisiac effects. It's also a diuretic and should be taken with care.

Although burdock often grows in natural areas, wild burdock should not be harvested. The plant looks like belladonna nightshade plants, which are toxic. Before consuming burdock root, confirm its source; purchase plants and seeds to plant in a tea garden from a reputable retailer.

Grow burdock in shade and alkaline soil. It produces a large taproot, which you can use after the first season, but you cannot harvest the seeds of the biennial until the second season. Use dried burdock root to make tea. Dig out the taproot with a shovel—avoid pulling the plant because the root will break—and then scrub the roots and allow them to dry, which could take several days. Dried roots will be crisp and pliable. You can also dry burdock root in a food dehydrator.

Burdock has a strong, earthy flavor that is best brewed with honey or stevia to improve the taste. Limit consumption of burdock root tea to one cup per day.

🍵 For the best brew:

Add 1 teaspoon (5ml) of dried, chopped burdock root to 2 cups (480ml) of boiling water and steep for fifteen minutes. Strain the roots before drinking.

CHICORY
(*Cichorium intybus*)

- **Zones**: 3 to 8

Chicory might be best known as a caffeine-free alternative to coffee, but you can also use the roots to make tea. The showy perennial is native to Europe, Asia, and Africa and often considered a weed in the United States (it's listed as an invasive species in Colorado and New Mexico). A taproot that grows beneath the surface of the soil, chicory spreads quickly. Harvest it in the fall, before the first frost.

Despite being a fibrous—and fiber-rich—root, chicory has a creamy flavor. The creaminess pairs well with spices like nutmeg, cinnamon, and cloves.

Chicory grows up to 4 feet (1.2m) tall and 2 feet (60cm) wide, producing green to russet-colored stems and light blue (sometimes white or pink) flowers with daisy-like petals that close in the afternoon. The flowers bloom in May and June and again in September and October. Due to its aggressive nature, chicory tolerates poor conditions, including drought and poor soil, but it does not like hot, humid climates. Harvesting the root kills the plant, so you will need to replant chicory annually.

Studies have linked chicory, also known as succory, to a host of health benefits, from reducing inflammation and improving gut health to easing constipation. Chicory might trigger an allergic reaction in those sensitive to ragweed. It can also lower blood sugar; therefore, those with diabetes should use it with caution.

🍵 For the best brew:

Wash and dry the root and chop it into small pieces. (A milk-like sap is released when the fleshy taproot is cut.) Add 1 teaspoon (5ml) of chicory root to 1 cup (240ml) of water and let steep for at least five minutes. Strain the root before drinking.

GINGER
(*Zingiber officinale*)

■ **Zones:** 9 to 12

A tropical plant native to South Asia, ginger can be grown in the United States if the conditions are right. The perennial prefers hot, humid conditions. Growing ginger in a container is ideal, so you can transfer the plant indoors to extend the growing season.

The plant will die if left outdoors when temperatures drop below 50°F (10°C).

You can start ginger from a root purchased at the supermarket. Cut the root into 1- to 2-inch (2.5cm to 5cm) sections; leave them for twenty-four to forty-eight hours (long

🫖 For the best brew:

Grate 2 tablespoons (30ml) of fresh ginger or a 2-inch (5cm)-thick slice of ginger root and add it to 2 cups (480ml) of boiling water. Let it steep for five minutes or longer. Ginger is pungent; adding 1 teaspoon (5ml) of sweetener, such as honey or agave, can make the flavor less overwhelming.

enough for the ends to form thin scabs). Choose an area with partial to full shade and plant the root about 1 inch (2.5cm) below the surface of the soil. It takes time for a good-sized rhizome (root) to develop, so allow ginger to grow for a full season before harvesting.

Give ginger room to grow. The plants can grow up to 4 feet (1.2m) tall and spread just as wide, so be sure to provide enough space in the garden. As a garden specimen, ginger is unremarkable—it produces oblong leaves on opposite sides of thick stems—but the root of the ancient spice makes a pungent and healing tea.

Revered for its health benefits, ginger has been a staple of alternative medicine for centuries. The pungent powerhouse is used for nausea and morning sickness, muscle aches, motion sickness, indigestion, and viruses such as colds and flu.

GINSENG
(*Panax quinquefolius*)

- **Zones**: 4 to 8

Prized among foragers, ginseng is a sought-after root used to lower inflammation, boost mood, support the immune system, increase energy levels, and lower blood

sugar. Ginseng is native to the Ozark and Appalachian regions in the eastern United States, but wild populations are endangered—and, in some regions,

extinct—because of overharvesting. The roots were being shipped to China, where populations of their native species, *Panax ginseng*, weren't robust enough to meet demand for the medicinal herb.

This popular herb should not be harvested from the wild but grown in the garden instead. The three-stalked perennial grows up to 15 inches (38cm) tall; small greenish-white flowers with a delicate fragrance appear on the stalks in June and July. When the flowers die, clusters of red berries appear.

Ginseng is difficult to grow. It prefers higher elevations and cooler climates. Choose a location in partial to full shade; under tree canopies, similar to its habitat in the wild, is ideal. Provide moist, neutral soil; if the soil is too acidic, ginseng will die.

Be prepared to wait for a cup of ginseng tea. It takes up to ten years for ginseng roots to grow large enough to be harvested. Avoid damaging the roots during harvest.

For the best brew:

Add 2 tablespoons (30ml) of fresh or dried ginseng to 1 cup (240ml) of boiling water. Let steep for five minutes and strain before serving. Add 1 teaspoon (5ml) of honey to offset the bitterness.

LICORICE
(*Glycyrrhiza glabra*)
■ **Zones**: 7 to 10

In Greek, *glykys* means "sweet" and *rhiza* means "root." The licorice flavor in this perennial—sometimes called sweetwood or sweet root—is used to flavor candies and confections and can be brewed into a flavorful tea.

Licorice is a member of the pea and bean families. There are twenty species of licorice; *Glycyrrhiza glabra* is a popular medicinal plant that is used for sore throats, menstrual cramps, and ulcers. Too much licorice root is associated with heart issues and high blood pressure.

The perennial herb is native to Europe, Africa, and Asia. Pairs of leaves grow on opposite sides of long stems, and light blue-purple flowers (similar in appearance to sweet peas) bloom in the summer. It's the underground rhizomes, which grow up to 3 feet (90cm) long, that make this plant special. The roots are reported to be fifty times sweeter than sugar and can be used fresh or dried to make a sweet tea. It can take two years before the root is established enough to be harvested; commercial growers wait up to four years before harvesting.

Grow licorice in sun to part shade. It prefers sandy, slightly alkaline soil. Licorice is easy to grow from seeds or propagated from cuttings.

♨ For the best brew:

Add 2 teaspoons (10ml) of dried, chopped licorice root to 1 cup (240ml) of boiling water and let steep for three to five minutes. Strain the roots before drinking.

VALERIAN
(*Valeriana officinalis*)

■ **Zones**: 4 to 7

Valerian appears to act as a sedative, making it popular as a sleep aid. The herb is also used to treat hot flashes during menopause, depression, stress, headaches, and muscle and joint pain. The calming compounds in the roots are so powerful that valerian is often viewed as an over-the-counter alternative to valium.

The evergreen scent and flavor in the leaves and roots makes it a popular food additive, but it can be perceived as strong. Pairing it with chamomile, lemon, or peppermint-flavored herbs can help mask the bitterness.

The perennial, also known as garden heliotrope, produces scented leaves and roots; white to pale pink flowers start blooming in June. It grows up to 5 feet (1.5m) high and 4 feet (1.2m) wide. Valerian grows best in full sun and damp locations, but it will also tolerate drier soils. Remove spent flowers to prevent valerian from self-seeding and taking over the garden.

Valerian is prized for the medicinal properties in its roots—and those healing benefits are strongest in the spring and fall. Accessing the root means uprooting the perennial. Dig up the plant, taking care not to harm the roots, and then hang the plant in a dark location until the roots are dried (it can take a few weeks). Once the roots are dried, clip them and store them in a container in a cool, dark place.

☕ For the best brew:

Mix ½ teaspoon (2.5ml) of dried valerian root with 2 cups (480ml) of boiling water and let steep for three minutes. Strain the roots before sipping. Add honey to reduce the bitterness.

GROW YOUR OWN SWEETENER: STEVIA

Stevia (*Stevia rebaudiana*) is a popular plant-based sweetener that makes an excellent addition to a tea garden. Stevia earned the nicknames "sweetleaf" and "sugarleaf" because the leaves are up to 300 times sweeter than cane sugar.

A perennial in zones 10 and 11 (and an annual in zones 9 and lower), stevia is native to South America and has been used to sweeten the local tea, yerba maté, for more than 1,500 years. The first commercial stevia-based sweetener was developed in the 1970s but not approved in the United States until the early 2000s. It's not allowed as a food ingredient; instead, it is labeled as a dietary supplement.

Stevia has long, slender leaves and produces tubular white flowers in July and August. It thrives in warm temperatures and moist, well-drained soil. It prefers full sun but will tolerate part shade.

Though it's sweet, this member of the aster family has no impact on blood sugar or blood pressure. While researchers believe that stevia is safe, provided it is consumed in moderation, some animal studies linked this sweet herb to lowered sperm production and increased risks of infertility and cancer.

For the best brew:

Fresh stevia leaves are sweet and can be used plucked right from the plant, but dried leaves are even sweeter. Leaves can also be ground in a food processor to create a fine powder that is used similarly to sugar. Both dried stevia and stevia powder can be stored through the winter.

CHAPTER 3

BREWING THE BEST TEA GARDEN

You don't have to be a landscape designer (or hire one) to grow a productive and beautiful tea garden. Choose plants based on their color, fragrance, space and light requirements, or healing properties, and just start experimenting. This chapter includes tips for best practices in cultivating and maintaining your tea garden, as well as eight suggested garden designs that can be tweaked based on your garden space.

Best Practices

While there are no hard-and-fast rules for planting a tea garden, following a few best practices will help your garden thrive.

Prepare the soil: Some plants will tolerate poor soil—I'm looking at you, oregano and rosemary—but most prefer a nutrient-rich mix to thrive. Dig down at least 12 inches (30cm) and work in a layer of compost. Rake the soil until it's well mixed and has a loose texture. If soil is compacted, water and oxygen cannot reach the roots. Many plants also prefer well-drained soil because it allows the water to flow through without puddling. Saturated soil can lead to issues such as root rot. Testing the pH of the soil with a kit from the home-improvement store can also provide guidance for soil amendments. For example, acidic soil can burn plants, but adding lime, which is alkaline, can help neutralize the soil.

Do not skimp on soil preparation. Be sure to rake your soil.

If necessary, add lime to help neutralize overly acidic soil.

Assess the location: How much sun does the garden get? Plants that require full sun need at least six hours of sun per day. Too little sun might hamper their growth. On the opposite end of the spectrum, plants that require partial to full shade might get leaf scald or wither and die if planted in a spot with too much sun. Look at soil drainage, too.

You can test the pH of your own soil with an at-home kit.

Be aware of how much sun each area of your garden will get throughout the year because different plants have different needs.

Tend the plants: A little TLC can help small seedlings grow into lush plants that will make countless cups of tea. In addition to keeping your garden watered (mornings and evenings when the sun isn't at its peak are the best times), pull weeds to prevent them from choking out the plants, and prune and thin plants as needed.

Pruning plants helps them grow and ultimately helps your harvest.

Water in the mornings and evenings.

Watch for pests: If you keep an eye out and spot pests early, you might be able to remove them by hand and simply squish them. Some pests, such as aphids and mites, can be eradicated with mild detergent and water. Mix 2½ tablespoons (37.5ml) of detergent with 1 gallon (3.8 liters) of water, fill a squirt bottle, and spray the leaves. If a more aggressive approach is needed, choose pesticides like neem oil, copper sulfate, and hydrogen peroxide that are approved for use in organic gardens. You'll want to steer clear of harsh chemicals because you'll be using the plants in tea you'll be imbibing.

Spray aphids and mites with a mix of mild detergent and water.

Think about garden structure: Planting directly into a new or existing garden bed is always an option. Often, though, soil quality is poor, so you may need to add amendments like peat moss, manure, grass clippings, and compost to boost soil health. Building a raised bed that you can fill with bags of nutrient-rich organic matter provides a good base for plants. Planting in containers is another good option—just make sure to use potting soil, not garden soil, because garden soil is heavier and can become compacted, preventing water from reaching the roots. Containers are also a great choice for herbs like mint that spread quickly and can take over the garden if not kept in check.

Raised beds allow you to precisely control the soil base in which your plants grow.

Containers are a suitable option for many plants.

Containers are recommended for mint because all kinds of mint can rapidly spread and take over the entire garden.

Avoid overharvesting: It may seem counterintuitive, but it's best to harvest the tender new growth, not the larger, more mature leaves. Young leaves offer the most flavor, and leaving the larger, lower leaves also helps promote vigorous plant growth—but don't pluck too many of those tender leaves. Overharvesting depletes supplies and, in the wild, can make it harder for plants to survive. If you're planning to make big batches of herbal teas, plant extra herbs and harvest smaller quantities from each.

City Living

Just because you live in an apartment or without access to a yard doesn't mean that you can't grow your own teas. You may be somewhat more limited by space and light, but you can still grow a ton of different plants for your brews, so don't be discouraged.

Garden Designs

Do you have specific needs or tastes that you want your garden to fulfill? Or do you just like the idea of thought-out themes? Whatever the case, I've prepared nine different plant layout suggestions for your garden. If you have the space, you could even create all eight of these gardens in different spots.

HANGOVER CURE TEA GARDEN

Forget the "hair of the dog." To recover from an evening of overindulgence, harvest hibiscus, parsley, lavender, and fennel—herbs that are known for easing the effects of a hangover—from the garden and brew a cup of tea. The fresh air while you're picking your ingredients will do you good, too!

Plants included: fennel (page 43), hibiscus (page 68), lavender (page 70), parsley (page 51)

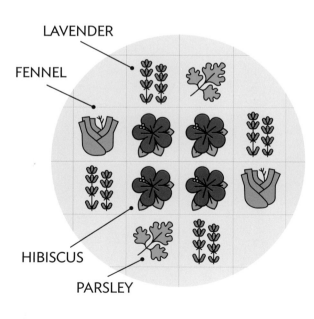

LAVENDER

FENNEL

HIBISCUS

PARSLEY

SLEEPYTIME TEA GARDEN

Having trouble falling asleep? Turn to the garden. A tea garden filled with chamomile, lavender, lemon balm, and echinacea can help you fall asleep fast—just remember to give echinacea the space it needs to thrive.

Plants included: chamomile (page 65), echinacea (page 67), lavender (page 70), lemon balm (page 47)

FATIGUE-FIGHTING TEA GARDEN

Need a burst of energy in the morning or a pick-me-up to fight the afternoon slump? A garden filled with holy basil, ginseng, chickweed, and licorice root can help. These healing herbs can give you the jolt of energy you need—*no caffeine required.*

Plants included: chickweed (page 39), ginseng (page 92), holy basil (page 44), licorice (page 93)

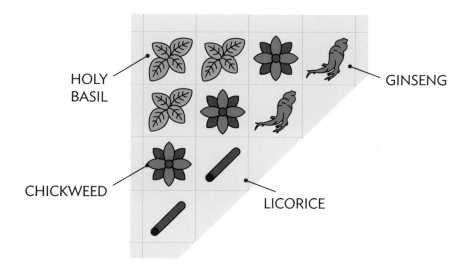

HOLY BASIL

GINSENG

CHICKWEED

LICORICE

RELAXING TEA GARDEN

What could be more relaxing than a steaming cup of tea? A steaming cup of tea brewed with red clover, purple passionflower, lavender, and St. John's wort, herbs known for having calming effects.

Plants included: lavender (page 70), purple passionflower (page 73), red clover (page 74), St. John's wort (page 60)

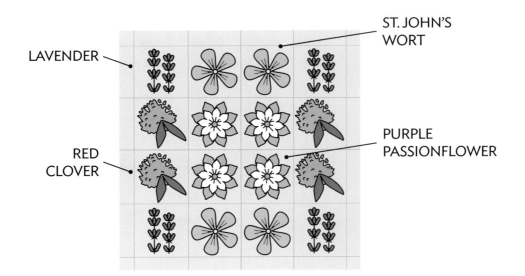

ST. JOHN'S WORT

LAVENDER

PURPLE PASSIONFLOWER

RED CLOVER

HEADACHE TEA GARDEN

Tea made from chamomile, peppermint, tufted violet, and trumpet honeysuckle can help ease the throbbing at your temples. Even better, these flowers and herbs are very easy to grow, so cultivating this tea garden won't cause any headaches.

   Plants included: chamomile (page 65), peppermint (page 53), trumpet honeysuckle (page 77), tufted violet (page 78)

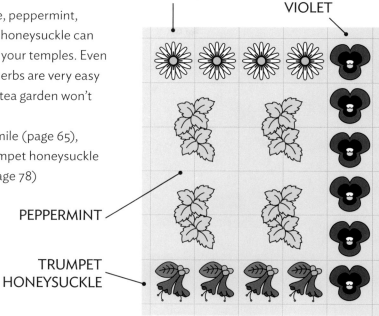

CHAMOMILE

TUFTED VIOLET

PEPPERMINT

TRUMPET HONEYSUCKLE

IMMUNE-BOOSTING TEA GARDEN

Not only has digging in the dirt been shown to have a positive impact on your immune system, brewing tea from spearmint, echinacea, trumpet honeysuckle, and purple passionflower—all hailed for their immune-boosting benefits—can keep you feeling well.

Plants included: echinacea (page 67), purple passionflower (page 73), spearmint (page 58), trumpet honeysuckle (page 77)

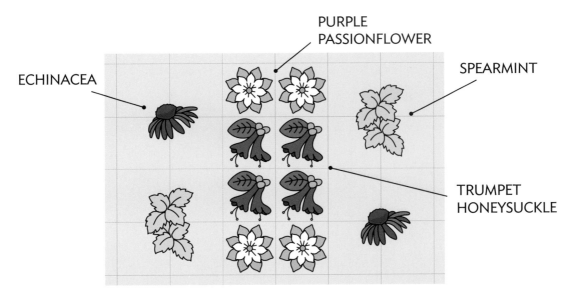

TUMMY TROUBLES TEA GARDEN

Ease digestive upset by growing a garden of fennel, ginger, rosemary, catnip, and thyme and using these medicinal herbs in a steaming cup of tea.

Plants included: catnip (page 38), fennel (page 43), ginger (page 90), rosemary (page 56), and thyme (page 61)

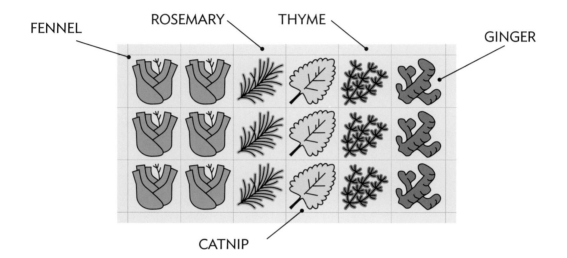

SHADE TEA GARDEN

No sun, no problem. Herbs such as apple mint, bee balm, lemon verbena, and stevia not only thrive in full to part shade, they can also be used to make (and sweeten) flavorful teas.

Plants included: apple mint (page 33), bee balm (page 35), lemon verbena (page 49), stevia (page 95)

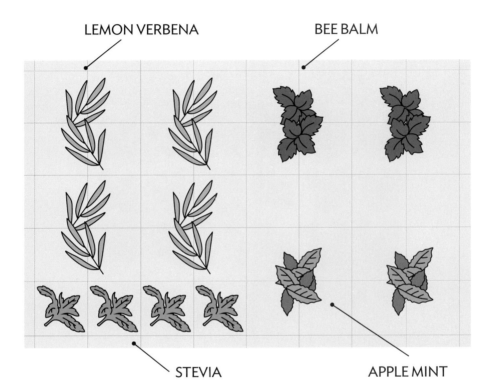

LOTS OF LEMON TEA GARDEN

Lemon is one of those rare flavors that is both soothing and uplifting. Although this garden is filled with lemony herbs, each offers a subtly different lemon flavor.

Plants included: bee balm (page 35), holy basil (page 44), lemon balm (page 47), lemongrass (page 48), lemon verbena (page 49)

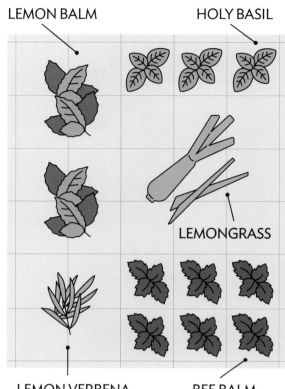

LEMON BALM

HOLY BASIL

LEMONGRASS

LEMON VERBENA

BEE BALM

CHAPTER 4

FROM CULTIVATION TO CUP: MAKING THE PERFECT CUP OF TEA

From the tools you use, to the brewing methods you choose, to the way you preserve your plants for future use, there is a surprising amount to know to masterfully make brews with your cultivations. In this chapter, you'll learn everything you need to ensure that each cup or pot you prepare is a symphony of taste, just the way you want it. Plus, at the end of the chapter, there are fourteen of my favorite personal recipes for you to try. Happy sipping!

Brewing

Brewing a cup of tea can be as simple as steeping a handful of fresh herbs in boiling water, but brewing a *great* cup of tea is a bit of a science. To make the best homegrown teas, first heed the following tips before you even heat up the water.

Steer clear of chemicals: Using sustainable methods to grow herbs, flowers, and fruit ensures that your tea ingredients are free of toxic pesticides and herbicides. Avoid harvesting tea ingredients such as dandelions, chickweed, and red clover in areas that might have been exposed to chemicals. Avoid growing or harvesting herbs near high-traffic areas; brake dust and other chemical residues can be hard to wash off.

Get educated: Not all foods are safe for steeping. Before heading out to the garden to pluck ingredients for tea, make sure that the plants are edible—and that you've correctly identified the species. If in doubt,

Don't be tempted to forage for plants like dandelions near high-traffic areas where they could be contaminated by brake dust and other chemicals.

These pokeweed berries look delicious, but they aren't safe to steep (or eat).

No matter how clean you keep your garden, wash everything you harvest before consuming it.

purchase a field guide to help you identify safe plants or take foraging classes to learn from a knowledgeable mentor. Talking to a naturopath or herbalist about which herbs might interact negatively with medications or health conditions is also a good idea before using food as medicine.

Wash everything: Thoroughly wash all foods plucked from the garden before adding them to the teapot.

Follow local laws: Foraging for wild foods can be a great way to supplement the ingredients growing in your garden, but remember that harvesting wild foods is illegal in some areas, including national parks. Check your local laws before you pluck.

There are many books out there to teach you effective and safe foraging skills, such as this one by David Squire.

Clean the equipment: Be sure to wash all of your equipment, including pans, drying racks, food dehydrators, teapots, and tea-ball strainers, thoroughly between uses. Cleaning the equipment not only eradicates bacteria but also ensures that the flavors don't transfer between brews, meaning that you will get the pure tastes you want.

Store safely: Store dried tea in airtight containers in a dark space (like a cupboard) for up to one year. See more information on drying your teas before storage on page 119.

Clean all equipment, including a food dehydrator (shown here), between uses.

Store harvested and dried plants in airtight containers, away from sunlight.

ESSENTIAL TOOLS FOR DIY BREWS

You can make tea with basic kitchen equipment, such as a sieve and a mug, but there are many other tools that can make DIY brewing a snap.

Kettle: Sure, you can boil water in a saucepan, but a kettle, whether an electric or stovetop model, has a lid and spout perfect for pouring hot water into a cup or teapot.

Measuring cups: Experiment with different amounts of tea leaves (both on their own and in blends) and take notes on which measurements lead to the perfect brew.

Mortar and pestle: These old-fashioned tools are ideal for crumbling dried leaves to make loose-leaf teas and tea blends.

French press: The plunger in this tool pushes the tea leaves to the bottom and the piping hot brew to the top—no straining required.

Tea-ball strainer: Filling a tea-ball strainer with loose-leaf tea is another way to avoid straining leaves before drinking tea. They come in many shapes.

Sieve: For larger batches of loose-leaf tea, a sieve is essential to separate the leaves from the steeped tea.

Tea bags: Package tea like the pros with tea filter bags. Look for unbleached options; the models with drawstrings are the easiest to use.

EQUATIONS FOR THE BEST BREWS

Depending on the type of tea you are brewing, you will want to hit a particular water temperature, use a set quantity of tea, and steep for a specific length of time. This will unlock the best, purest flavors of the tea. Some of the more expensive electric kettles allow you to choose the temperature. If you don't have such a kettle, use a glass thermometer.

Type of Tea	Water Temperature	Quantity	Steep Time
White	160–185°F (71–85°C)	1 tablespoon (15ml) of tea per cup (240ml) of water	2–3 minutes
Green	170–185°F (77–85°C)	1 teaspoon (5ml) of tea per cup (240ml) of water	3–5 minutes
Oolong	185–205°F (85–96°C)	1 teaspoon (5ml) of tea per cup (240ml) of water	1–3 minutes
Black	190–205°F (88–96°C)	1 teaspoon (5ml) of tea per cup (240ml) of water	3–5 minutes
Tisane	Any temperature	Depends on herbs	To taste

When stored properly, dried herbs are safe from bacteria and mold.

Preserving the Harvest

You could stick to brewing tea solely from fresh herbs, but learning how to dry them allows you to preserve the harvest and make garden-to-teacup brews all year long. Dried herbs are also safe from bacteria and mold and retain their flavor and potency for up to one year. For the best results, use one of the following three methods for drying herbs. For each, always wash herbs first and then pat them dry with a clean paper towel to remove as much moisture as possible. Once the herbs have dried, store them in glass jars with lids, and label the jars with the herb (or blend) and the date.

Air-drying: This low-tech method has worked for centuries. Harvest a bundle of herbs; tie the stems together with a twist tie; wrap the bundle with a mesh or muslin bag that is thin enough to allow air circulation while catching any falling leaves; and hang the bundle upside down. You can also place

Glass jars are a good option when storing teas.

herbs on a drying screen (an old, clean window screen is a good DIY option). Simply place a muslin cloth over the screen, line the screen with a single layer of herbs, and leave the herbs to dry. Depending on the moisture content, herbs can take several hours or several days to dry. Herbs are dried when they crumble easily.

Oven-drying: Choose the lowest heat setting possible—less than 180°F (82°C) is ideal because if the temperature is too high, the herbs will bake, not dry. Place a single layer of herbs on a cookie sheet and place it in the oven. Leave the oven door open a crack to allow air to circulate. Check the herbs every fifteen minutes. Low-moisture herbs, such as oregano, marjoram, and rosemary, will require less time than other herbs that have higher moisture content. Expect oven-drying herbs to take at least forty-five minutes; some will take much longer. Let herbs cool before handling them.

Dehydrating: Food dehydrators are excellent for drying herbs. While it's best to follow the instructions in the operating manual, as a general rule of thumb, preheat the dehydrator to 115°F (46°C) (higher if you live in a humid climate). Place herbs on trays in a single layer, making note of which herbs are on which trays; it can be hard to tell dried herbs apart. Set the timer. Expect it to take at least one hour—but potentially much longer—for the herbs to fully dry. Check them every fifteen minutes to monitor their progress. After you remove the herbs from the dehydrator, allow them to cool before handling.

Air-drying is a classic and almost foolproof method of preserving your harvest.

Make your oven into an herb dryer.

Using a food dehydrator can be an efficient way to dry herbs.

Morning is the best time to harvest herbs.

Air-drying herbs is a natural way to preserve their maximum flavor.

Don't be afraid to mix different teas and herbs together. You might hit upon a real winner!

Three Tips for a Great Cup of Tea

Harvest early: To seal in the flavor, cut herbs first thing in the morning. Use a sharp pair of shears to clip the leaves after the dew has dried but before the sun gets too hot; the heat draws out the natural oils that give herbs their flavor. Instead of letting herbs grow wild, harvest them often. Snipping a few sprigs or a handful of leaves serves as an informal pruning. Harvesting herbs before they start to flower keeps the energy in the leaves, which helps preserve their fresh flavors.

Dry herbs naturally: You can keep sipping the flavors of your labor all winter long by drying fresh herbs harvested in the summer. Lay the leaves on a towel in the hot sun until they turn crispy. The leaves must be dry enough to crumble; if there is any moisture left in them, they will get moldy. Once the leaves are dried, store them in glass jars in a cool, dry place.

Have fun: Growing the ingredients for tea is all about experimentation. Start with a few favorites; sample new plants; mix and match like a mad scientist and see what happens. Not all DIY blends will be a hit, but some flavor combinations might lead to surprisingly tasty teas.

Recipes

CILANTRO MINT TEA

These bright, citrusy flavors come together to create a refreshing cup of tea. Because both herbs are known to ease tummy troubles, cilantro mint tea is a great choice for an after-dinner brew.

Makes 1 to 2 servings.

- 1 tablespoon (15ml) fresh cilantro (coriander) leaves, packed
- 1 tablespoon (15ml) fresh peppermint leaves
- 2 teaspoons (10ml) orange peel (no white pith), coarsely chopped
- 1 teaspoon (5ml) fresh ginger, finely chopped
- 2 cups (480ml) water
- Honey to taste

Place the herbs, orange peel, and ginger in a cup. Gently crush with the back of a small spoon to release the essential oils. Bring the water to a boil. Pour hot water over the herb mixture and let it steep for five to seven minutes. Strain the leaves and stir in honey to taste.

LEMON BALM BLEND

Lemon is both calming and uplifting, making it a great choice if you're anxious or feeling blue. Before taking your first sip, breathe in the invigorating scent.

Makes 1 to 2 servings.

- ½ cup (120ml) fresh peppermint leaves
- ½ cup (120ml) fresh lemon balm leaves
- 2 cups (480ml) water

Place the peppermint and lemon balm leaves in a teapot. Bring a kettle of water to a boil and pour it over the leaves, leaving it to steep for three to five minutes. Strain the leaves before drinking.

PEPPERMINT RASPBERRY TEA

The sweetness of the raspberries balances the cool "bite" of the peppermint in this refreshing tea. Over ice, peppermint raspberry tea is a great thirst quencher, but the minty tea with a hint of sweetness can also be enjoyed hot.

Makes 3 to 4 servings.

- 1 handful fresh peppermint leaves
- 1 handful fresh raspberries
- 4 cups (960ml) water

Bring a kettle of water to a boil. Pour boiling water over the peppermint leaves and raspberries. Leave the brew to steep overnight. To drink, strain the leaves and berries and reheat, or pour the tea over a cup of ice.

CALENDULA SUN TEA

This old-fashioned process for "brewing" tea harkens back to a simpler time. Add a little honey to balance out the sometimes spicy flavor of the calendula flowers.

Makes 3 to 4 servings.

- 1 cup (240ml) fresh calendula flowers

- 4 cups (960ml) cold water

- Honey to taste

Fill a 2-quart (1.9-liter) jar with the fresh flowers and cold water; seal with an airtight lid. Choose a sunny day and leave the jar on a windowsill for at least eight hours. Strain the flowers and pour the liquid over ice.

REFRESHING HIBISCUS TEA

Hibiscus is a tropical flower with a tart, refreshing flavor. Pour it over ice and imagine sipping it on the beach—or brew a cup as a pick-me-up after a day of working in the garden.

Makes 6 to 8 servings.

- 1½ cups (360ml) dried hibiscus flowers
- 1 cup (240ml) sugar
- 2 teaspoons (10ml) grated ginger
- Squirt of lime juice
- 8 cups (1.9 liters) water, separated

Boil 4 cups (960ml) of water. Add the hibiscus flowers and ginger to the boiling water and let rest for one hour. Strain the flowers and then add the sugar, remaining 4 cups (960ml) of water, and a squirt of lime juice. Stir and serve over ice.

IMMUNE-BOOSTING BLEND

Starting to feel under the weather? The sweet and pungent flavor combination in this healing tea can help. If the ginger is too pungent, cut the quantity or add honey to taste.

Makes 3 to 4 servings.

- 1 tablespoon (15ml) dried echinacea
- ½ cup (120ml) fresh strawberries
- 1 tablespoon (15ml) dried rose hips
- 1 tablespoon (15ml) grated ginger
- 4 cups (960ml) water

Bring the water to a boil and then add echinacea, strawberries, rose hips, and ginger. Let the tea steep for at least thirty minutes. Strain the herbs, pour into a warm mug, and sip.

SLEEPYTIME TEA

The subtly sweet flavors and heady scents of the herbs in this best-before-bed brew can help you drift into dreamland.

Makes 3 to 4 servings.

- 1 tablespoon (15ml) dried lemon balm
- 1 tablespoon (15ml) dried peppermint
- 1 tablespoon (15ml) dried rose petals
- 1 tablespoon (15ml) dried lavender leaves
- 1 teaspoon (5ml) fennel seeds
- 4 cups (960ml) water
- Honey to taste

Bring the water to a boil and then add lemon balm, peppermint, rose petals, lavender leaves, and fennel seeds. Let the tea steep for five minutes. Strain the herbs, pour the tea into a warm mug, add honey to taste, and sip.

TROPICAL ICED TEA

This sweet iced tea has a bit of a bite thanks to the tartness in the lemon juice. It's the perfect brew for a hot summer day.

Makes 3 to 4 servings.

- ½ cup (120ml) fresh pineapple sage leaves, packed
- ½ cup (120ml) pineapple juice, poured into ice-cube trays
- 1 teaspoon (5ml) lemon juice
- 4 cups (960ml) water
- Honey to taste

Boil the water, add the pineapple sage leaves and lemon juice, and leave to steep for twenty minutes. Strain the leaves, pour into a glass, add honey to taste, and add three to five pineapple-juice cubes.

LAVENDER LEMON TEA

Although these herbs are opposites when it comes to their effects—lavender is calming and lemon is uplifting—the iconic flavors pair perfectly in a tea that has a sweet floral essence.

Makes 3 to 4 servings.

- 1 tablespoon (15ml) dried lavender leaves

- 1 tablespoon (15ml) dried lemon balm leaves

- 4 cups (960ml) water

Bring the water to a boil, add the lavender and lemon balm, and steep for five minutes. Strain the herbs, pour into a warm mug, and serve. To enjoy iced, let it steep overnight, strain, and pour over ice.

CITRUS LIFT TEA

Need a pick-me-up? The distinct citrus flavors in these popular herbs blend perfectly for an uplifting (and aromatic) cup of tea.

Makes 3 to 4 servings.

- 1 tablespoon (15ml) fresh lemon verbena leaves
- 1 tablespoon (15ml) fresh lemon balm leaves
- 1 tablespoon (15ml) fresh bee balm leaves
- 4 cups (960ml) water

Boil the water; add the lemon verbena, lemon balm, and bee balm; and steep for three to five minutes. Strain the leaves, pour the tea into a warm mug, and serve.

WEEDY BREW

Think twice before ridding the garden of weeds. The earthy flavors of chickweed, dandelion, and red clover—not to mention their healing properties—make a unique savory tea.

Makes 3 to 4 servings.

- 2 tablespoons (30ml) fresh chickweed
- 2 tablespoons (30ml) fresh dandelion flowers
- 2 tablespoons (30ml) fresh red clover
- 4 cups (960ml) water
- Honey to taste

Thoroughly wash all of the ingredients. Boil the water in a small saucepan; add the chickweed, dandelion flowers, and red clover; and let steep for ten minutes. Strain the leaves and flowers and pour into a warm mug. Add honey to taste.

TUMMY TROUBLES TEA

Not feeling well? All of the ingredients in Tummy Troubles Tea have been shown to ease digestive upset, and, thanks to the hint of sweetness in the herbs, the tea will go down like a spoonful of sugar.

Makes 3 to 4 servings.

- 1 tablespoon (15ml) dried echinacea flowers
- 1 tablespoon (15ml) fresh bee balm leaves
- 1 tablespoon (15ml) fresh anise hyssop leaves
- 1 tablespoon (15ml) fennel
- 4 cups (960ml) water

Boil the water and then add the purple coneflowers, bee balm leaves, anise hyssop leaves, and fennel. Steep for three to five minutes. Strain the leaves, pour the tea into a warm mug, and serve.

HEADACHE RELIEF TEA

Sipping a cup of Headache Relief Tea and inhaling the aroma of the herbs can help ease a tension headache. The peppermint adds a little tang to the sweet floral flavor, making this a cup of tea you'll want to drink even when you don't have a headache.

Makes 3 to 4 servings.

- 1 tablespoon (15ml) fresh peppermint leaves
- 1 tablespoon (15ml) fresh chamomile flowers
- 1 tablespoon (15ml) fresh apple mint leaves
- 4 cups (960ml) water

Boil the water; add the peppermint leaves, chamomile flowers, and apple mint leaves; and steep for three to five minutes. Strain the leaves, pour the tea into a warm mug, and serve.

MMM MINT ICED TEA

Hot or iced, mint tea is nice, and these three mint varieties, each with their own distinct flavor, blend perfectly in a tangy but not-too-sweet cup of tea.

Makes 3 to 4 servings.

- 1 teaspoon (5ml) fresh spearmint leaves
- 1 teaspoon (5ml) fresh peppermint leaves
- 1 teaspoon (5ml) fresh lavender mint leaves
- 4 cups (960ml) water

Boil the water, add the leaves to the water, and leave to steep in the refrigerator overnight. Strain the leaves, pour the water over ice, and sip. You can also enjoy this tea hot by boiling the water, adding the ingredients, and steeping for ten minutes. Strain the leaves, pour into a warm mug, and serve.

PLANT HARDINESS ZONE MAPS

The United States map shown here is a modified reproduction of the official USDA Plant Hardiness Zone Map. To view the official map, which includes the "a" and "b" subzones, go to *https://planthardiness.ars.usda.gov*.

AVERAGE ANNUAL EXTREME MINIMUM TEMPERATURE
1976–2005

TEMP (°F)	ZONE	TEMP (°C)
−60 to −50	1	−51.1 to −45.6
−50 to −40	2	−45.6 to −40
−40 to −30	3	−40 to −34.4
−30 to −20	4	−34.4 to −28.9
−20 to −10	5	−28.9 to −23.3
−10 to 0	6	−23.3 to −17.8
0 to 10	7	−17.8 to −12.2
10 to 20	8	−12.2 to −6.7
20 to 30	9	−6.7 to −1.1
30 to 40	10	−1.1 to 4.4
40 to 50	11	4.4 to 10
50 to 60	12	10 to 15.6
60 to 70	13	15.6 to 21.1

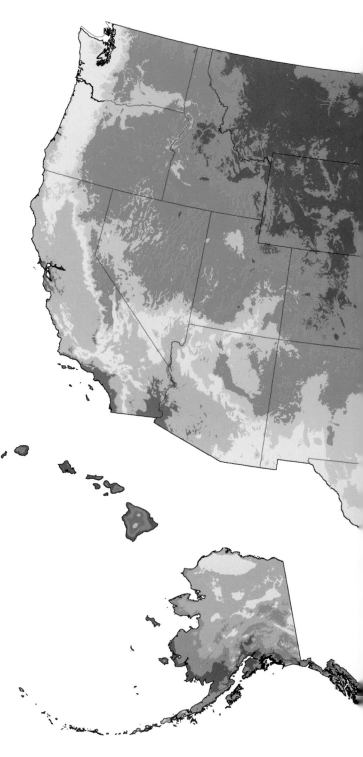

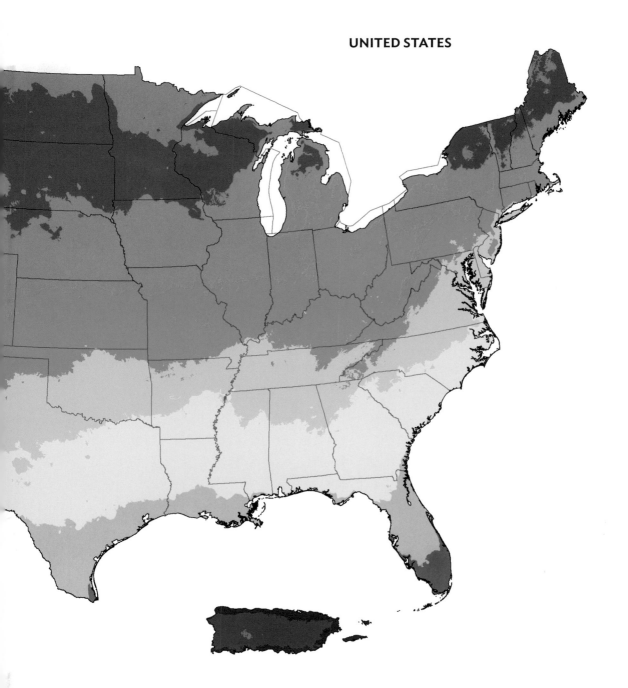

From the United States Department of Agriculture (USDA) website, *www.planthardiness.ars.usda.gov.*

EXTREME MINIMUM TEMPERATURE ZONES

TEMP (°F)	ZONE	TEMP (°C)
-70 to -65	0a	-56.7 to -53.9
-65 to -60	0b	-53.9 to -51.1
-60 to -55	1a	-51.1 to -48.3
-55 to -50	1b	-48.3 to -45.6
-50 to -45	2a	-45.6 to -42.8
-45 to -40	2b	-42.8 to -40.0
-40 to -35	3a	-40.0 to -37.2
-35 to -30	3b	-37.2 to -34.3
-30 to -25	4a	-34.3 to -31.7
-25 to -20	4b	-31.7 to -28.9
-20 to -15	5a	-28.9 to -26.1
-15 to -10	5b	-26.1 to -23.3
-10 to -5	6a	-23.3 to -20.6
-5 to 0	6b	-20.6 to -17.8
0 to 5	7a	-17.8 to -15.0
5 to 10	7b	-15.0 to -12.2
10 to 15	8a	-12.2 to -9.4
15 to 20	8b	-9.4 to -6.7
20 to 25	9a	-6.7 to -3.9

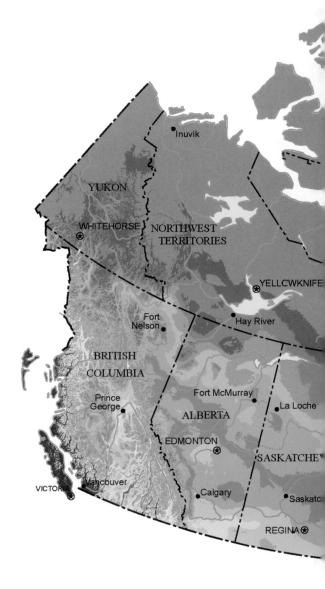

CANADA

Resolute

Cambridge Bay

N U N A V U T

IQALUIT

NEWFOUNDLAND AND LABRADOR

Rankin Inlet

Kuujjuaq

Happy Valley-
Goose Bay

Churchill

ST JOHN'S

MANITOBA

Chisasibi

Q U É B E C

P E I
Î-P-É

N B
N-B

CHARLOTTETOWN

FREDERICTON

ONTARIO

QUÉBEC

HALIFAX

NNIPEG
Brandon

Kenora

NOVA SCOTIA

Thunder
Bay

Montréal

Sault
Ste Marie

OTTAWA

TORONTO

From Natural Resources Canada website, *www.planthardiness.gc.ca*

RESOURCES

PLANT AND SEED SUPPLIERS

American Meadows

877-309-7333

www.americanmeadows.com

A Vermont-based online retailer that has been supplying gardeners with high-quality seeds and perennials for more than thirty years.

Camellia Forest Nursery

919-968-0504

www.camforest.com

Offers an incredible selection of *Camellia* varieties, including several varieties of *Camellia sinensis*. Ships seeds or mature plants nationwide. The North Carolina nursery offers tours of its tea gardens and hosts workshops and tea tastings.

Johnny's Selected Seeds

877-564-6697

www.johnnyseeds.com

A respected supplier of seeds and tools since 1973. Sells a huge selection of organic, non-GMO seeds.

Mountain Rose Herbs

541-741-7307

www.mountainroseherbs.com

Huge selection of bulk herbs (dried) and tea supplies.

Renee's Garden

888-880-7228

www.reneesgarden.com

Specializes in heirloom, non-GMO, organic seeds and open-pollinated varieties.

Richters

800-668-4372

www.richters.com

Specializes in selling and shipping fresh herbs and herb seeds.

Seed Savers Exchange

563-382-5990

www.seedsavers.org

Specializes in open-pollinated, heirloom seeds.

The Thyme Garden Herb Company

541-487-8671

www.thymegarden.com

Offers herb seeds, dried herbs, and herbal tea blends.

TEA SUPPLIERS

Arbor Teas

734-994-7698

www.arborteas.com

Source of tea bags for loose-leaf teas.

English Tea Store

877-734-2458

www.englishteastore.com

Offers teapots, mugs, infusers, strainers, and other tea accessories.

TeaSource

651-788-9971

www.teasource.com

Sells a selection of kettles, tea scoops, infusers, and honey dippers.

RECOMMENDED READING

A Brief History of Tea by Roy Moxham (Running Press, 2009)

For All the Tea in China: How England Stole the World's Favorite Drink and Changed History by Sarah Rose (Penguin Books, 2011)

The Story of Tea: A Cultural History and Drinking Guide by Mary Lou Heiss and Robert J. Heiss (Ten Speed Press, 2007)

The Tea Enthusiast's Handbook: A Guide to Enjoying the World's Best Teas by Mary Lou Heiss and Robert J. Heiss (Ten Speed Press, 2010)

Tea: History, Terroirs, Varieties (third edition) by Kevin Gascoyne, François Marchand, Jasmin Desharnais, and Hugo Américi (Firefly Books, 2018)

ABOUT THE AUTHOR

Jodi Helmer is a North Carolina-based journalist who writes about food, gardening, farming, and the environment. She has written for *National Geographic Traveler, Hobby Farms, FarmLife, The Guardian, Smithsonian.com, Sierra.com,* and *Scientific American* and is the author of six books, including *Protecting Pollinators: How to Save the Creatures that Feed Our World.* When she's not writing, she works in the garden and raises bees.

PHOTO CREDITS

FC = front cover; BC = back cover; t = top; b = bottom; l = left; r = right; m = middle

The following images are credited to Shutterstock.com and their respective creators: FC: Maya Kruchankova; BCt: Scisetti Alfio; BCb: Irina Burakova; 2: nika-lit; 6 br: Africa Studio; 6 background: Elovich; 7 background: Elovich; 8: Rustle; 10–11: Snowbelle; 12 right: GreenArt; 13 t: beeboys; 15 t: Ingus Kruklitis; 15 b: Hari Mahidhar; 16 b: spatuletail; 17 b: zhu difeng; 18: Rajesh Narayanan; 19: nixki; 20–21: Ratchanee Sawasdijira; 22 t: Sanit Fuangnakhon; 23 t: Elena Odareeva; 23 b: Sitthichai Kaewkam; 24: Maridav; 25: topimages; 27 tl: isak55; 27 tr: Zapylaiev Kostiantyn; 27 b: Louno Morose; 28: Iryna Denysova;

29: slawomir.gawryluk; 30: Nataliia Pyzhova; 31: KPG_Payless; 32 t: Carlos Rondon; 32 b: mizy; 33 t: marilyn barbone; 33 b: Manfred Ruckszio; 34 t: SnelsonStock; 34 b: NazarPro; 35 t: shansh23; 35 b: luisami; 36 t: Swapan Photography; 36 b: Alter-ego; 37 t: BUSINESS-CREATIONS; 37 b: Sakcared; 38 t: emberiza; 38 b: Zigzag Mountain Art; 39 t: spline_x; 39 b: Przemyslaw Muszynski; 40 t: Aedka Studio; 40 b: 336food; 41 t: D_M; 41 b: Akvals; 42 t: Cozine; 42 b: simona pavan; 43 t: shansh23; 43 b: lzf; 44 t: PosiNote; 44 b: PosiNote; 45: Pinh To; 46 t: Skyprayer2005; 46 b: Klemens Pohl; 47 t: Scisetti Alfio;

47 b: Martina Roth; 48 t: Aimmi; 48 b: Nannie_iiuu; 49 t: Scisetti Alfio; 49 b: JurateBuiviene; 50 t: Scisetti Alfio; 50 bottm: sasimoto; 51 t: Scisetti Alfio; 51 b: pkorchagina; 52 t: Ruttawee Jai; 52 b: Stephen Orsillo; 53 t: Scisetti Alfio; 53 b: Zigzag Mountain Art; 54 t: Martina Osmy; 54 b: Skyprayer2005; 55: I. Rottlaender; 56 t: Richard Peterson; 56 b: pilialoha; 57 t: Scisetti Alfio; 57 b: Ahmet Yasti; 58 t: anmbph; 58 b: ChWeiss; 59 t: Imageman; 59 b: waldenstroem; 60 t: Scisetti Alfio; 60 b: Medwether; 61 t: Bjoern Wylezich; 61 b: NANCY AYUMI KUNIHIRO; 62 t: LianeM; 62 b: lightrain; 63 t: Marc Lee; 63 b:

Gabriela Beres; 64 t: ZoranOrcik; 64 b: Africa Studio; 65 t: oksana2010; 65 b: Itija; 66 t: Scisetti Alfio; 66 b: snowturtle; 67 t: spline_x; 67 b: Nada Sertic; 68 t: Scisetti Alfio; 68 b: Marques; 69 t: Scisetti Alfio; 69 b: Tukaram.Karve; 70 t: Hortimages; 70 b: Cora Mueller; 71 t: haraldmuc; 71 b: dadalia; 72 t: osoznanie.jizni; 72 b: Peter Radacsi; 73 t: Nyvlt-art; 73 b: Ezume Images; 74 t: Ziablik; 74 b: Grigorii Pisotsckii; 75 t: matka_Wariatka; 75 b: Malykalexa; 76 t: spline_x; 76 b: Mariola Anna S; 77 t: Gino Santa Maria; 77 b: Prokuronov Andrey; 78 t: kzww; 78 b: Anquetil Anthony; 79: Ole Schoener; 80 t: Eskymaks; 80 b: Mark Herreid; 81 t: Imageman; 81 b: Nick Pecker; 82 t: Olga_Ionina; 82 b: Manfred Ruckszio; 83 t: Santi S; 83 b: tmpr; 84 t: Manfred Ruckszio; 84 b: Volcko Mar; 85 t: Hortimages; 85 b: Manfred Ruckszio; 86 t: Ilizia; 86 b: De Jongh Photography; 87 t: ANGHI; 87 b: neil langan; 88 t: Boonchuay1970; 88 b: Ihor Bondarenko; 89 t: Nata Studio; 89 b: Ihor Hvozdetskyi; 90 t: NUM LPPHOTO; 90 b: pilipphoto; 91 tr: StudioPhotoDFlorez; 91 bl: Doikanoy; 91 br: picturepartners; 92 t: Jiang Zhongyan; 92 b: Igor Cheri; 93 t: limpido; 93 b: Manfred Ruckszio; 94 t: shansh23; 94 b: Ole Schoener; 95 t: Scisetti Alfio; 95 b: joloei; 96–97: Lee Yiu Tung; 98 left: kryzhov; 98 right: richsouthwales; 99 t: Sergey Kamshylin; 99 b: Peter Turner Photography; 100 left: mythja; 100 right: Purino; 101 t: Four-leaf; 101 b: Jamie Hooper; 102 tl: pixfix; 102 tr: kridsada tipchot; 102 b: Shannon West; 103 right: Olinchuk; 104 b: Jacob Lund; 105 b: mirzamlk; 106 b: almaje; 107 b: Sirintra Pumsopa; 108 b: Alexander Raths; 109 b: Maya Kruchankova; 110 b: junichi arai; 111 b: Toa55; 112–113: Valentina_G; 114 t: Vladimir Konstantinov; 114

b: samray; 115 t: Rawpixel.com; 116 t: Olga Popova; 116 b: Dmitry Galaganov; 117 t: July Prokopiv; 117 mt: DiAnna Paulk; 117 mb: Africa Studio; 117 b: Fotobyjuliet; 118 t: Anna Hoychuk; 118 m: Pixel-Shot; 118 b: Pavel Andreyenka; 119 t: Geo-grafika; 119 b: Milante; 120 t: angelakatharina; 120 m: YURENIA NATALLIA; 120 b: julie deshaies; 121 t: Alexander Raths; 121 m: Kwang Meena; 121 b: Mariya Siyanko; 122: Africa Studio; 123: Africa Studio; 124: 5PH; 125: Madeleine Steinbach; 126: MarieKaz; 127: ILEISH ANNA; 128: Irina Burakova; 129: Heike Rau; 130: Kasabutskaya Nataliya; 131: Heike Rau; 132: Snowbelle; 133: LianeM; 134: Africa Studio; 135: Alexey Lysenko; 140–141: CoralAntlerCreative; 142 background: nika-lit

The following plant icons are also credited to Shutterstock.com and their creator, Happy Art: fennel 103, 109; parsley 103; lemon balm 104, 111; holy basil 105, 111; purple passionflower 106, 108; peppermint 107; spearmint 108; rosemary 109; thyme 109; ginger 109; lemon verbena 110, 111; bee balm 110, 111; apple mint 110

The following plant icons are credited to Flaticon.com and their respective creators: lavender 103, 104, 106: dDara from www.flaticon.com; hibiscus 103: Freepik from www.flaticon.com; chamomile 104, 107: Freepik from www.flaticon.com; licorice 105: Freepik from www.flaticon.com; St. John's wort 106: Freepik from www.flaticon.com; lemongrass 111: dDara from www.flaticon.com

The following plant icons are credited to Llara Pazdan: echinacea 104, 108; ginseng 105; chickweed 105; red clover

106; tufted violet 107; trumpet honeysuckle 107, 108; catnip 109; stevia 110

The following images are credited to their respective creators: 9: author; 142 center: author; 5 background and 122–135 border background: author; 17 top: Llara Pazdan; 26: JusTea; 136–137: United States Department of Agriculture (USDA), https://planthardiness.ars.usda.gov; 138–139: Natural Resources Canada, www.planthardiness.gc.ca; mug on all "For the best brew" boxes: designed by Freepik.com; spine pattern: designed by Freepik.com; 5 pattern and 122–135 border pattern: designed by Freepik.com; 10, 20, 96, 112 pattern: designed by Freepik.com

The following images are faithful photographic reproductions of two-dimensional works of art that are in the public domain in the United States, their countries of origin, and other countries depending on the copyright term: page 12 left: page of *De Materia Medica*, dated circa 512, from the illuminated manuscript *Vienna Dioscurides*, author unknown; page 13 bottom: illustration of Saichō, dated 1905, from the book *The Cult of Tea [O culto do chá]* by Venceslau de Morais, illustration by Yoshiaki Utagawa; page 14 top: painting titled "Arrival of JC van Neck," dated circa 1592–1661, by Cornelis Vroom; page 14 bottom: painting titled "Portrait of a lady drinking tea," dated circa 1737–1807, by Niclas Lafrensen; page 16 top: lithograph titled "The Destruction of Tea at Boston Harbor," dated 1846, by Nathaniel Currier

INDEX

Note: Page numbers in **bold** indicate plant primary discussions, and page numbers in *italics* indicate recipes.